THE COACHING HABIT

TINY

HABITS

Discover The Little Things You've Been Missing So Far In Your Life

Martinez Thomas

Table of Contents

PART 1

Chapter 1:

Start Working On Your Dreams Today

When did you get up today? What was your day like? What did you achieve today? Did any of that matter?

Maybe it didn't because you don't have any dreams to work towards, or maybe that you've forgotten what they are altogether.

To have a dream is to have a direction in life. To have a dream means you have something bigger than yourself that you want to achieve.

Everyone gets at least one chance in their life to actually go and pursue that dream, but few recognize that until it is too late. It is too late to regret when you are on your deathbed wondering what could have been. That is when it is too late to work on your dreams. When you have no more time left.

The Moment to start working On your dreams is right here right now.

We repeat our failures every day but never learn. We get depressed every day but never communicate. We get bullied every day, but never fight back. Why?

Is it because we can't do it? No, Definitely Not! We can do it whenever we want. We can do it today. We can do it the next minute. We just lack Ambition!

Every day someone achieves something big. Some more than often, others maybe not their whole life. But the outcome is **not** determined by **fate**, but with **Effort**.

All the billionaires you see today started out with a few dollars just like you and me. They just had the guts to pursue their dream no matter what the cost is. They all had a vision of something bigger. They went full throttle even when everyone around them expected them to fail. Even when they met with struggles that hit them harder than the last, they were still focused on the dream. Never did they once lesson the effort.

No two persons are born the same. Not the same face, color, intelligence, or fate. But what's common for every human being is the built-in trait to strive for a goal once they are determined enough. Doesn't matter if it's food for the next meal or success for the times to come.

The struggle is real, it always was, it always will be. The world wouldn't be what it is today if it weren't for the struggle man has gone through over the centuries. The struggle is the most real definition of life in this world. But that doesn't mean it's a bad one.

Our parents struggled to make us a better person. They put in their best effort to watch us succeed in our dreams. Their parents did the same for them and their parents before them.

This is what makes life a cycle of inherited struggle and hardships. Nobody asks to struggle through a hard life, but we can all turn the hard life into a meaningful one. The life that we all should expect to eventually achieve only if we keep the cycle running and if we keep putting in the effort.

How then do we actually work towards our dreams? By focusing on the things that matter each and every day, again and again, until that mountain has been conquered. Don't forget to enjoy the journey, because it could well be the best part of the trip up top.

You never know what the next moment has in it for you. You can never predict the future, but you can always hope for a better one. You only get the right to hope if you did what was meant to be done today. It's your lawful right to reap the fruit if you took care of sowing the seeds faithfully and diligently all through the year.

The motivation behind this continuous grind of time in search of that Dream lies in your past. You cannot achieve those dreams until you start treasuring the lessons of your past and become a person who is always willing to go beyond.

You can't simply depend on hope to get something done. You have to reach the point where start obsessing over that goal, that thing, that DREAM. When you start obsessing, you start working, you start seeing the possibilities and you just keep going. If you don't get up then you WILL miss the moment. The moment that could have made all the difference in the world. If you don't act upon that impulse, you might never get that inspiration ever again. And that will be the moment you will always regret for the rest of your life.

Remember that your whole life is built on millions of tiny decisions. A decision to just act on one of those moments can transform your life completely. These moments often test you too. But only for an inch more before you find eternal glory. So don't wait for someone else to do it for you. Get up, buckle up, and start doing. Because only you Can!

Chapter 2:

9 Habits of Highly Successful People

Success comes to people who deserve it. I bet you have heard this statement quite a few times, right? So, what does it mean exactly? Does it mean that you are either born worthy or unworthy of success? Absolutely not. Everyone is born worthy, but the one thing that makes some people successful is their winning habits and their commitment to these habits.

Today, we will learn how to master ten simple habits and behaviors that will help you become successful.

1. Be an Avid Learner

If you didn't know, almost all of the most successful people in the world are avid learners. So, do not shy away from opportunities when it comes to learning. Wake up each day and look forward to learning new things, and in no time, I bet you will experience how enriching it really is. Also, learning new things has the effect of revitalizing a person. So, if you want to have more knowledge to kickstart your journey in the right direction, here are some things that you can do - make sure to read, even if it is just a page or two, daily. It could be anything that interests you. I personally love reading self-help books. If you are not that much of a reader, you can even listen to a podcast, watch an informative video, or sign up for a course. Choose what piques your interest, and just dive into it!

2. Failure is the Pillar of Success

Most people are afraid to delve into something new, start a new chapter of their lives, and chase after their dreams – all because they are scared to fail. If you are one of those people who are scared to fail, well, don't be! Because what failure actually does is prepares you to achieve your dream. It just makes sure that you are able to handle the success when you finally have it. So when you accept that failure is an inevitable part of your journey, you will be able to plan the right course of action to tackle it instead of just being too scared to move forward. Successful people are never scared of failure; They just turn it around by seeing it as an opportunity to learn.

3. Get Up Early

I bet you have heard this a couple of thousand times already! But whoever told you so was not lying. Almost all successful individuals are early risers! They say that starting the morning right ensures a fruitful day ahead. It is true! Think about it, on the day you get up early, you feel a boost of productivity as compared to when you wake up late and have to struggle against the clock. You will have plenty of time and a good mood to go through the rest of the day which will give you better outcomes. All you have to do is set up a bedtime reminder. This is going to make sure that you enough rest to get up in the morning instead of snoozing your alarm on repeat! Not a morning person? Don't worry. I have got you covered! Start slow and set the alarm 15 minutes before when you usually wake up. It doesn't sound like much, eh? But trust me, you will be motivated to wake up earlier when you see how much difference 15 minutes can make to your day.

4. Have Your Own Morning Ritual

Morning rituals are the most common habit among achievers. It will pump you up to go through the day with a bang! You just have to make a routine for yourself and make sure to follow it every day. You can take inspiration from the morning routines of people you look up to but remember it has to benefit you. So you might be wondering, *What do I include in the ritual?* I would suggest you make your bed first thing in the morning. This might not sound as great a deal, but hey, it is a tested and approved method to boost your productivity. It is even implemented in the military. Doing this will motivate you as you get a sense of achievement as you have completed a task as soon as you woke up. After that, it could be anything that will encourage you, such as a walk, a workout session, reading, journaling, or meditating.

5. Stop Procrastinating

From delaying one task to not keeping up with your deadlines, procrastination becomes a deadly habit. It becomes almost unstoppable! Did you know, most people fail to achieve their dreams even if they have the potential just because of procrastination? Well, they do. And you might not want to become one of them. They say, "Old habits die hard," true, but they do die if you want them to. Procrastination has to be the hardest thing we have to deal with, even though we hey created it in the first place. Trust me, I speak from experience!

So what do you do to stop this? Break your task into small bite-sized pieces. Sometimes, it is just the heaviness of the task that keeps us from doing it. Take breaks in between to keep yourself motivated.

Another thing that you can do is the "minute rule." Divide your tasks by how much time they take. The tasks that take less than 5 minutes, you do it right then. Then you can bigger tasks into small time frames and complete them. Make sure you do not get too lost in the breaks, though!

6. Set Goals

I cannot even begin to tell you how effective goal setting is. A goal gives you the right direction and motivation. It also gives you a sense of urgency to do a task that is going to just take your productivity level from 0 to 10 in no time!

So how do you set goals? Simple. Think about the goals you want to achieve and write them down. But make sure that you set realistic goals. If you find it difficult, don't worry. Start small and slow. Start by making a to-do list for the day. You will find out soo that the satisfaction in ticking those off your list is unbelievable. It will also drive you to tick more of them off!

7. Make Your Health a Priority

Health is Wealth. Yes, it is a fact! When you give your body the right things and make it a priority, it gives you back by keeping you and your mind healthy. I bet you've heard the saying "You are what you eat," and by "eat," it does not simply mean to chew and swallow! It also means that you need to feed your body, soul, and mind with things you want them to be like. Read, listen, learn, and eat healthy. You could set a goal to eat clean for the week. Or workout at least for 10 minutes. And see for yourself how it gives you the energy to smash those goals you've been holding off! Also, great news – you can have cheat days once a week!

8. Plan Your Day the Night Before

"When you fail to plan, you plan to fail." People who succeed in life are not by mere coincidence or luck. It is the result of detailed, focused planning. So, you need to start planning your way to success too. Before you sleep tonight, ask yourself, *What is the most important thing that I have to do tomorrow?* Plan what assignments, meetings, or classes you have to complete. Planning ahead will not only make you organized and ready, it also highly increases your chances to succeed. So, don't forget to plan your day tonight!

9. Master the Habit Loop

Behavioral expert, BJ Fogg, explains that habits are formed around three elements: Cue, Routine, and Reward. Cue is the initial desire that motivates your behavior. Routine is the action you take. And the reward is the pleasure you gain after completion. So why am I telling you all of this? Because this habit loop is how we are wired. It is what motivates us. We seek pleasure and avoid pain. And you can use this loop to your advantage! Let's say you want to finish an assignment. Think of the reason why you want to. Maybe you don't want to fall behind someone or want to impress someone. It could be anything! Now time for you to set your rewards. It could be eating a slice of cheesecake or watching an episode of your favorite series after you've finished. Rewards motivate you when you slack off. Play around until you find a combination that works best for you. You will also need a cue; it could be anything like a notification on your phone, an email, or simply your desire. You can set a cue yourself by creating a reminder.

Habits are what make a man. I hope you follow these habits and start your journey the right way to becoming successful in life.

Chapter 3:

10 Habits of Lewis Hamilton

One thing is certain about Lewis Hamilton: he is a legend. He is a four-time Formula One World Champion who knows how to win on the track and in life. He is widely lauded as one of the best drivers of his generation, if not all time. In 2008, he became the youngest champion in history, winning the final turn of the season's final race.

He raced in Formula One for three decades, winning a record-equalling seven world championships, triple-figure pole positions, and a knighthood. You're surely aware that Lewis oozes driving talent, but there's much more to Hamilton than what he does behind the wheel. Here are the ten habits of Lewis Hamilton.

1. Executes Under Pressure

Racing drivers like Lewis must control and remain calm despite driving at speeds up to 230 miles per hour in a sports car that may reach temperatures of 50 degrees. With limited space and vision, you can imagine how hectic it is for him to composure himself to adapt, make split-second decisions, and win.

2. Keep Your Eyes on the Price

As a child, Lewis always wanted to be a race car driver. He even met his future boss, Ron Dennis, as a toddler and promised him that he'd be racing his cars in the future. With his attention and persistence, he was able to turn that goal into reality. How determined and focused are you in attaining your goals? Keep your eventual aim in sight at all times!

3. Technology Is Everything

Formula one racing is a technology-driven sport in which a minor flaw in the car can alter the race's outcome. Hamilton and his team are always ahead of others with well-researched data for optimizing his performance. To place your content in the driver's seat for success, it must be easily available, properly categorized, and in the proper format, which is why the platform you deal with must be intelligent, smart, and dependable.

4. Discipline Pays Off

Lewis Hamilton is one of the world's most disciplined athletes. While some people may not consider Formula one racing to be a sport in which you must be in peak physical condition to be successful, Lewis treats his physical fitness as a shrine for his mental health lucidity as mental health is key to racing. His commitment to healthy food and consistent training has helped him win 43 Formula One races throughout his career.

5. Put in the Effort

Lewis is all about dedication to excellence. "You start training in December, start testing at the end of January and through the entire month of February, and then you go to the season," he explained. You're always on the move. How committed are you to attain your most important goals? Small steps lead to big steps, and big steps lead to bigger steps.

6. Dispatch, Adapt and Enhance

When Lewis achieves something, he celebrates his victory debriefing, analyses his performance, and learns how they may have improved their racing plan. Lewis Hamilton is the best because of his relentless, determined pursuit of perfection. It would be best to always debrief with a reliable team, react to problems and develop your techniques, and stay ahead of the competition.

7. Physical and Mental Health First

Lewis is always trying to stay optimistic and healthy for his body, mind, soul, and spirit. It's hard to step back from doing something you love most but look at the bigger picture. Instead of grumbling or worrying about the future, step back and examine yourself-accessing and confronting your current issues.

8. Keep the Right People

While it appears that you get to tour the world and explore in Formula One, you spend more time alone. Lewis spends most of his time with Angela-his best friend, trainer, and physiotherapist. She exudes positive energy and always keeps him strong and motivated, so he can focus on remaining competitive.

9. Don't Gauge Yourself Against Others.

Lewis doesn't consider other drivers in terms of inspiration, motivation, or anything else. He's always sailing his boat towards becoming the best he can be. Devote your energy and time in improving yourself for yourself, not for others.

10. Self-Belief Is Key

Rosanna once asked Lewis, "Is there ever a time when you doubt your own abilities?" "No," Lewis said. Without delving too deeply into this, it's a given that you should believe in yourself in the same way Hamilton does.

Conclusion

Lewis Hamilton relentless determination towards being the best is what keeps him a champion. And just like him, always work towards perfecting what you are good at.

Chapter 4:

Gravitational Leadership

Leadership.

It's not about position it is about disposition. It is not a title it is a role. A role you can take on from any place. Even if you are at the lowest point in the hierarchy – you can still lead. Leadership is not about being on the top rung, it is about holding ladders for others. It is not about having the most authority either. When a battalion went on a mission authorised by the King, the battalion did not have the King's authority, only his approval. Yet within them someone could still rise and lead the others. The beginning of your leadership is making decisions and taking action that gets approved by the people in authority. In doing that you will get noticed and over time trusted as an advisor. Sometimes the way you think and conduct yourself will enable you to lead people above you before you get any opportunity to lead people below you.

Because leadership is gravity.

Gravity does not push us downwards. It is not a force that comes from above us and holds us back.

Firstly, gravity does not push it pulls. Pulling involves leading by example and drawing people to you by virtue of your character. The good decisions that you make, the beneficial actions that you take, start to bundle together as a mass of admirable quality under your name. And gravity is just a reflection of mass. The more you engage and go all-in the faster that mass will grow – and with it your gravity will.

But gravity is not just something that attracts the people below you. Gravity doesn't pull downwards on a 2D plane, it pulls towards a centre. The people who are on the same level as you should be led by you as well. Not only that but you should be influencing the people above you. Not in such a way that you suck up to them but in a way that you stand out. Not necessarily even with the intention of climbing the ladder. Leadership must always be about leading in the space that you are without leaning towards the space you want to be. Allow promotions or advancements to flow naturally – if you try to force them then you will be detracting from your gravity and ultimately end up worse off.

Lastly, gravity does not hold people back, it keeps them grounded. Gravity is the force that enables us to walk forward, to move while retaining control. People who have been to space can testify to the lack of control experienced without gravity and the dangers therein. The markings of a leader is someone who is able to keep people grounded to the mission while still giving them freedom of movement. Gravity does not inhibit progress it gives it a better framework to work within. It allows people to pursue things with passion while staying within the borders of a greater purpose.

Such is the makings of a leader.

Chapter 5:

10 Habits of Joe Biden

There is a proclamation that portrays leaders as people who meet their times. Probably the contrary appears true for US president Joe Biden. Time has met the man!

Since its inception, President Joe Biden's political career has been distinguished by a seismic lurch, from setbacks to triumphs. Biden has served in the United States Senate for 36 years and as Vice President for two terms under Barack Obama's administration. All along, he became the ultimate political ally and the nation's unofficial top consoler.

His third run for the White House was unfolding just as expected: a front running falls into oblivion. Then came Super Tuesday. What can you grasp from the man whose fate just intervened for greatness?

Here are 10 habits of Joe Biden.

1. He Works With Objectives

According to Matthew Crayne, an organizational psychologist, and professor, one of Joe Biden's strengths in handling the Covid-19 vaccine rollout is that he has maintained a clear set of objectives that are easily communicated and understood. Essentially, clear objectives will disclose your program's success and setbacks.

2. Don't Bluff

Given the heated relationship between the United States and Russia over the years-from Crimea to Syria to election involvement to ransomware-you might think Biden's meeting with Russian President Putin earlier this year was a bluff. Truth is, he went to Geneva that early in his presidency with specific goals in mind; to establish the terms of their relationship.

3. A Waver? No

Biden hasn't wavered in his vision for the future, and he continually emphasizes that progress is being made, but the mission isn't finished. As a leader, employing this habit in your strategies will help impart a sense of accomplishment and urgency into the population, both of which are vital in driving long-term collective action.

4. He Embraces His Mistakes

Joe Biden's past journey to the White House was rocky, from allegations tarnishing his academic credentials to controversy over handling Clarence Thomas Supreme court case. However, he didn't derail in admitting his mistakes, a character that could later rank him as the most trustworthy politician according to a 2015 CBS News/New York Times survey. Embracing your mistakes is a crucial foundation of your every worthwhile goal.

5. Sets Good Examples

As a leader, your work is to influence those you lead by acting accordingly. While fighting the spread of the Corona Virus, President

Biden has leveraged his office's status and influence to conduct symbolic gestures. Wearing a mask during public appearances and publicly getting his dose of the vaccination. This may appear apparent and expected, but still is influential for collective action.

6. Get Stuff Done

The only thing that should matter is the outcome, and so, for example, if you recall when President Obama said, Joe's going to do the Recovery Act and its Sheriff Joe, and nobody messes with me. The guys in the House and Senate applauded, saying, "Yeah, that's Joe. And we like Joe like that."

7. Empathy Defines Him

As a leader, how you respond to adversity is a guide to your character. Biden is moved by his personal tragedies in consoling the masses. His impassionate statement the day before his inauguration to the relatives of the 400,000 Americans killed by Covid-19 says it all.

8. Actions Are Better

Holding back from acting prevents you from exploring your capabilities and abilities. President Biden's choice to meet with Russian President showed that he was a man of actions. That is, he attended the meeting in good faith, seeking to pave the way for normative accords, which in turn could provide Americans and their allies with a way forward.

9. Be Humble

Under Trump's leadership, the US devolved into a dangerous place for its profound racial gap. Biden's seeming humility, hard-won and life-learned, lends itself well to reconciling the problem. More often, it is your hard humbling that will assist you in reaching a point where you can make the necessary changes.

10. You're Not Bigger Than Your Role

The job of a leader encompasses more than just you. It's never about you; it's always about the people, the nation. Power is something you must acquire, and not given to you by your role. The best leaders like President Biden have an unrivaled desire to lead others in a cause greater than themselves.

Conclusion

The measure of a person is not how frequently he falls but how swiftly he gets up. Failure is unavoidable at some times, but quitting is inexcusable. With all of its ups and downs, Biden's habits will teach you some essential leadership lessons.

Chapter 6:

<u>10 Habits of Jeff Bezos</u>

As you know, your lifestyle choices can make or break your success. It began in a basement and has since grown into a well-known online shopping app. Jeff Bezos' brainchild, the "Everything Store," is a platform where people get online deals. Commonly known as Amazon.com, the "Everything Store" is billion dollars' worth.

Jeff Bezos' habits vary from what to read to dealing with stress, which he phrases as "laugh a lot." Bezos, the self-made millionaire and Amazon CEO, is one of the world's wealthiest persons. But, what got him there? His natural aptitude for business got him there. Moreover, his habits are key to his achievements.

Here are ten business-oriented Jeff Bezos' habits for innovative-minds upkeep.

1. Customer-Centric Approach

Unlike most of the business, Bezos and Amazon have in decades ignored a "profitable" approach to doing business; instead, he invests in a customer-centric approach. Although at some point Amazon got chastised by publishers for allowing the laity to evaluate books, Amazon encouraged its consumers to share their comments, whether critical or negative.

An incentive that created a Clientele review platform which is why Amazon.com is today's most trusted e-commerce platform. Keeping a soundtrack of your customers means that you're taking good care of them.

2. Make Your Plan Based on Things That Will Not Change

While trading your brands-be it, lipstick, tractor seats, e-book readers, or data storages, make bigger plans with these constants: Provider your clientele with a broader selection scope, lower pricing, and rapid, dependable delivery.

3. Create Your Own Rules

If you despise writing essays, Amazon might not be the place for you. Amazon made it a rule early that anyone who wishes to suggest a new concept must first condense their views into a six-page booklet.

Before making any decisions, everyone concerned, must read and analyze the six-pager. And also, according to Bezos, "no team should be so large that two pizzas won't be enough." When your organization is far larger to be fed by two pizzas, divide it into fewer independent units of your own liking and capabilities to compete for limited resources while making your customers happy.

4. Work Backwards to What Your Customers Require

Customers' desires, rather than drivers' preferences, have shaped the specifications for Amazon's significant new projects, such as the Kindle tablets and e-book readers. So if your clientele doesn't want something, let it go, even if it means dismantling a once-powerful department.

5. Master the Art of Failure

Bezos's Amazon recruited many editors to produce book and music evaluations but later decided to use user feedback instead. A move that failed miserably.

Such blunders, according to Bezos, are a normal part of your innovative life, as long as you're on a learning reality, failure is sometimes positive. To succeed as an innovator, means that you are in for such flaws as taking risks, failing at a point while tucking your sleeves for a changes.

6. Make Informed Choices or Decisions

If you did know that Amazon began as a bookstore, well, here you have it! Bezos' product decisions are always a product of well thought logics and factual data rather than incidental incentives. Your product decision should be knowledgeable, and reading is knowledge.

In a nutshell, books are the ideal driver for e-commerce. Because nearly every aspect of commerce and customer behavior can be quantified, and almost all choices are based on data. Meetings are about metrics, not tales from customers!

7. You Are Willing To Be Misinterpreted for a Long Time

Many of Bezos-Amazon's initiatives appear as money-losing distractions. Which severally send the company's stock price down and earns the wrath of focal analysts. A five-to-seven-year financial plan is acceptable if your new initiatives make strategic sense to you.

8. Don't Mind the Competition

If your business is imitating and engrossed in what others are doing, then you're off Jeff Bezos' innovative strategies. In truth, client service should always come first. Just as Amazon Prime, succeed in your innovative plans while satisfying your clientele-base.

9. Don't Try To Be a Blockbuster

Your present success does not guarantee your future relevance. Consider the fate of Blockbuster Video and accept the fact that your industry advances with time, and will never hold similar standing as of now. Pay close attention to evolving state of affairs as you lead the change rather than reacting to it.

10. Ditch Complexity

Startups are characterized by rapid decision-making and innovation. However, as a company grows, it is frequently delayed by complexity. This suffocates innovation. Just like Bezos, always treat your company as a start-up at the cutting edge.

Conclusion

Following Jeff Bezos uniqueness will not guarantee you $100 billion. But you'll still set yourself up for a more prosperous future with your company endeavors if you maintain this proactive, forward-thinking approach.

Chapter 7:

10 Habits of Taylor Swift

Well-versed pop star isn't the only description for the "American Sweetheart" Taylor Swift- She's a woman with many talents and abilities. As a world-famous singer-songwriter, accomplished businesswoman, and fitness guru, Swift has risen to become one of the world's most renowned celebrities.

She signed her first record deal at the age of 15, has been nominated for over 500 awards, has won 324, and has sold over 50 million albums. Such success did not simply land to her automatically. As per the new Netflix documentary Miss Americana, Swift's growth is a journey of countless disappointing and challenging life and career lessons.

Here are 10 habits of Taylor Swift that can enrich your life and career path.

1. Certainty

Getting to where you want to be in life credits a clear vision. With a sense of clarity, you can pave the way to reach that destination.

Since the day she started her career in music, Taylor Swift has been clear on what she wanted. From the very young age she has served to steer her decision making, and enjoyed every bit of it.

2. Focus on the Brighter Side

Taylor Swift has had a share of public scandals, tabloids exploitation, and people who aimed at tarnishing her name with controversy. It is irrelevant whether they are justified or not, she continues to produce and thrive in her positive space. Just like Taylor Swift, develop an urge to always working past the ruins while strengthening your optimistic moods.

3. You Have No Control Over What Happens

The incident at 2009 VMAs with Kanye West fuelled Swift's desire to prove that her talent is undeniable. You'll learn from the Concert's footage performing her most critically acclaimed song, "All Too Well", that she's was not up to changing what people would eventually say about her but was only concerned with respecting her work ethic. Make your response to criticism a reflection of respect for your hustle!

4. Credit Your Success to Having a Niche

In the entertainment business, and with successful people like Taylor Swift, each one has their unique niche/speciality that sets them apart from everyone else. Major deeply on what makes you unique and what brought you there as your storyline is only for you to tell.

5. Courage Is the Secret to Longevity

Taylor went from being a trial for sexual assault, which she won the case, to her mother ailing from breast cancer and brain tumour to all the publicized stunts she had been through. Despite the challenges, she managed to produce indisputably remarkable projects. Just like Taylor, your confidence, resilience, brilliance, work ethic, and steadfast trust in your process will definitely garner appreciation and respect.

6. Own Your Power

Taylor Swift not only has power, but she also owns it. Following Scooter Braun and Scott Borchetta incident, Taylor was not scared to jeopardize her image or face the consequences of speaking up against something she honestly believed was unfair.

There are always risks to speaking out, but sitting silence may be far riskier. In some circumstances, being silent may endanger your opportunity to manage a project or receive a promotion or increase.

7. Develop Your Support System

Nurture your relationships if you'd like to gain more influence. Even though you are not on the same scale as Taylor Swift, maintained friendships influences your world. Listen to them if you want them to listen to you.

8. Follow Your Heroes

Taylor Swift started her profession at a young age. Her childhood was fraught with difficulties but had motivation from her idols, whom she followed their advice. If you adore someone who influences your life path, emulating two or three things from them pays off.

9. Be Influential

Taylor's success in the music industry has been her driving force in influencing other people. You don't have to have her numbers to be impactful. When you devote your time and energy to becoming productive, influential stats and metrics will follow you.

10. Maintain a Healthy Lifestyle

Being a celebrity doesn't mean that Swift's healthy lifestyle is about trendy diets and strange eating habits that dominates the entire Hollywood culture. According to PopSugar, Swift eats salads, nutritious sandwiches, yoghurt and hit the gym regularly during the week.

Conclusion

You don't have to be Taylor Swift, but you can learn from her. Increase your influence, cultivate your network, develop credibility, wield your authority, focus on positivity, resilience is vital, and feel free to stand your ground as you work on your uniqueness.

Chapter 8:

Playing To Your Strengths

Have you ever asked yourself why you fail at everything you touch?

Why you seem to lack behind everyone you strive to beat?

Why you can't give up the things that are keeping you from achieving the goals you dream?

Has anyone told you the reason for all this?

You might wonder about it all your life and might never get to the right answer. Even though you stare at the answer every day in the mirror.

Yes! It's you! You are the reason for your failures.

You are the reason for everything bad going on in your life right now.

But you are also the master of your life, and you should start acting like one.

When the world brings you down, find another way to overcome the pressures.

Find another way to beat the odds.

Adverse situations only serve to challenge you.

Be mentally strong and bring the world to your own game.

Show the world what you are.

Show the world what you are capable of.

Don't let anyone dictate to you what you should do.

Rather shape your life to dictate the outcome with your efforts and skills.

You can't always be wrong.

Somewhere, and somehow, you will get the right answer.

That will be your moment to build what you lost.

That will be your moment to shut everyone else and rise high in the silence of your opponents.

If you don't get that chance, don't wait for it to come.

Keep going your way and keep doing the things you do best.

Paths will open to your efforts one day.

You can't be bad at everything you do.

You must be good at something.

Find out what works for you.

Find out what drives your spirit.

Find out what you can do naturally while being blind-folded with your hands tied behind your back.

There is something out there that is calling out to you.

Once you find it, be the best at it as you can.

It doesn't matter if you do not get to the top.

You don't anything to prove to anyone.

You only need one glimpse of positivity to show yourself that you have something worthwhile to live for.

Always challenge yourself.

If you did 5 hours of work today, do 7 tomorrow.

If you run 1 mile today, hit 3 by the end of the week.

You know exactly what you are capable of.

Play to your strengths.

Make it your motto to keep going every single day.

Make a decision.

Be decisive.

Stick with it.

Don't be afraid because there is nothing to fear.

The only thing to fear is the fear itself.

Tell your heart and your mind today, that you can't stop, and you won't stop.

Till the time you have the last breath in your lungs and the last beat in your heart, keep going.

You will need to put your heart out to every chance you can get to raise yourself from all this world and be invincible.

You have no other option but to keep going.

To keep trying until you have broken all the barriers to freedom.

You are unique and you know it.

You just need to have the guts to admit that you are special and live up to the person you were always meant to be.

Take stock of yourself today.

Where are you right now and where do you want to be?

The moment you realize your true goal, that is the moment you have unlocked your strengths.

Live your life on your terms.

Every dream that you dream is obtainable.

And the only way is to believe in yourself.

To believe that you are the only thing standing in the way of your past and your future.

Once you have started, tell yourself that there is no return.

Dictate your body to give up only when you have crossed the finish line.

Start acting on every whim that might get you to the ultimate fate.

These whims are your strength because you have them for a purpose.

Why walk when you can run?

Why run when you can fly?

Why listen when you can sing?

Why go out and dine when you can cook?

The biggest gift that you can give to yourself is the mental satisfaction that you provide yourself.

You are only limited to the extent you cage yourself.

The time you let go will be your salvation. But you have to let go!

Chapter 9:

10 Habits of Larry Page

These days, children learn to google before they stroll, and a considerable part of the credit goes to Larry Page, the largest and most popular search engine one of the biggest innovators of our time. Larry Page, alongside his co-founder Sergey Brin, founded what has grown into one of the world's largest empires: the Google-search engine.

Nobody can simply ignore it: everybody else enjoys Google -apart from libraries. Page, could later step as CEO of Google to manage Alphabet, a technology company making waves across several industries. His success and conviction in what became the world's search engine set him apart from the start.

Here are ten worth mentioning Larry page's success habits for your success path lessons.

1. Pay Attention to Your Gut

If you're great in what you do, always respect your gut. Decisions are frequently made in haste due to time constraints, and if you have a gut sense that your choice is correct, you should go with that gut feeling. You may succeed or fail, but trusting yourself is pivotal for your well-being.

2. A Clear Vision

One key factor in Larry Page's success is knowing where he wanted to go, knowing where you want to go getting there much more accessible. Define your purpose in a single sentence to ensure that you truly understand what you want to achieve; if you can't, your goal isn't clear enough.

3. Focus on Your Strengths

When it comes to getting your things done quickly, you need to know where your strengths are. However, in some instances, you'll need to work on your weaknesses. This way, be sure of generating your finest work ever.

4. You Wouldn't need A Big Company to Make Your Idea a Reality

Google, Amazon, Apple, and Disney have in common is that all began in a garage with few resources but big dreams. So you only need to gamble on it, believe in your idea and go forward with determination to achieve your goals even if you lack the essential means at the time.

5. Allow Your Dreams To Direct Your Actions

All of your activities will become a lot easier to take after you've discovered your calling. All is required is your effort put in realizing your goals.

When you know what you genuinely want in life, the way to get there becomes a little clearer. Of course, there will always be ups and downs, but it is simpler to know what you are going for.

6. Don't Delegate, Do It Yourself

Most go-getters struggle with delegating work to others when they don't have the time to devote to them. Many leaders learn to let go, but Page was resistant to this change in his natural management approach early in his career. Make every effort to hasten the process. Though the verdict on the efficiency of this managerial approach is still out, it worked in Page's favour. Instead of wasting your efforts delegating, continue doing what you are incredibly great at.

7. You're Working on Changing the World

According to Larry's page, you're doing the right thing if your thing is benefiting the people. For your business to work well, the problems are solved, and demands met. Find a loophole in your society; let it count if you'll be part of the solution.

8. Learning Is Continuous

Larry Page once remarked, "the main things in life are to live, learn, and love." So follow your curiosity and take risks in your endeavours. Don't give up on your ambitions.

Nothing brings you more joy than reaching your goals and realizing your dreams; believe in your dreams because they may be able to sustain you for the long haul.

9. You Are Trust-Worth-People Have Trust in You

It would help if you won the trust of others, in this case, your audience-before they would believe in you. So focus on your audience's demands, maintain a presence on social networks where your target audience is, and carry out various actions to gain the trust of your potential clients, such as providing quality material or providing excellent customer service.

10. You are Respectful

People are your company's most valuable asset, and you should never lose sight of this. If you treat your staff with the same respect that you do your clients and potential clients, you will notice that they will treat your firm with the same regard.

Conclusion

In 2012, while still Google's Ceo, Larry Page told his investors, "whatever you can imagine is possible. Comfort is the worst friend a successful business can have, therefore avoid it at all costs and try to put some effort into every work you perform and every goal you seek. As your everyday work is exciting, could you keep it going? No holding back!

Chapter 10:

Focus – The Art of Alignment

Focus. A buzzword in the workspace. Everyone wants to have focus and keep focus. If you want it, you gotta understand it. Focus is not some abstract notion that comes and goes as it pleases. It only seems like that because you haven't learnt the rhythm of focus. Do you know what lures it in? Do you know what keeps it there once it comes?

Because at its core, focus is quite simple. If we look at a laser, we see a focussed beam of light, how? Lasers are concentrated light waves, in order for it to work the waves have to be coming from the same base, be going in the same direction, and be almost perfectly in sync.

Let me tell you that if you need to know who you are and what you want, because otherwise nothing will be coming from the same base. Everything that you do should stem from knowing who you are and who you want to be. If you know those two things then you start to bring everything into that bigger picture, you start every activity from that foundation.

If you want to be a professional athlete, then you go to your office job knowing that this is just a means to support your training and future career. You know that the better you perform there the closer you become to financial freedom and the more you can invest time into the thing you want to become. Not only will that motivate you to push through the mundane, but you will find constant fulfilment because everything you do will seem to bring you closer to your goals. Even if they are not related at all. If you are looking to become the CEO of a big company then you take the time to focus on cleaning your house because you cannot expect to bring order outside of your home if you do not have control within it.

Your first step to focus is finding your base and your direction, knowing who you are and who you want to be. Then you bring everything in sync with that. Because when everything flows in the patterns of your passion, focus is inevitable.

What about a camera? They focus by shifting the lens towards and away from the film. This means the light converges before or directly on the film, or it doesn't get to converge at all. When light converges all the points of it line up in a way that produces a clear picture. The art of photography is finding positioning it in such a way that what you want to capture is focussed. If you want to capture first place, if you want to get that promotion, whatever you want to do. You need to be able to adjust your focus so that the things you want are clear, and everything else blurs slightly into the background. Blurring does not distort your vision, it brings clarity to the primary focus. It ensures the desirable image of the future is sharp which means allowing the obstacles to blur into the process. When your focus is right, you don't get tempted by distractions. You see the bigger picture in light of your goals, not the deviations from them.

PART 2

Chapter 1:

Motivate Yourself

Motivation is a multibillion dollar industry.

There are many great motivational materials to help keep you motivated.

Some of the motivational material is great and should be studied and applied but this kind of motivation is what I call push, which is a good start, but in combination with pull motivation,(your personal why and reason), you can reach your goals faster.

With the use of videos, books , audio material and concentrating on your reasons, the sky really is the limit.

Using what works for you, which may be different than what works for others.

Motivation is very much personal to you.

Work with what pulls you and pushes you to reach your goals on record time.

Pushing and pulling everyday until your dream becomes reality.

The pull is your WHY , the big reason for taking action in the first place.

The pull is the motivations that effect you personally, and the big fire that will help your dream burn , even through the storms and the rain.

Using the push motivators in conjunction to maximize your motivation on all fronts.

Create as much of your dream around you as you can with what you have right now to make it seem more real.

Pictures , music , videos, foods, smells , clothing.

Whatever you can do to create it now.

The engine to drive you there may not have arrived yet, but don't close the factory, work on the interior and bodywork, because your engine is on the way.

You know what you want, you know the first steps, take them in confidence, not fear.

If the dream is here, it is already real if you just believe and move towards it.

With motivation , self determination and faith you have already won the race before it has even begun.

Setting up the ideal environment for the garden of your life to flourish.

Strengthen the desire, strengthen the belief.

Motivation in the mind without belief in the heart will only lead to disappointment.

Your why must be something close to the heart for you to endure the tribulations of champions.

Your motivations must be clear and personal.

Defining your purpose, often money alone will not make us happy.

The money must have a greater personal purpose to bring you happiness.

Giving often feels more rewarding than recieving.

As living a truthful life is more rewarding than decieving.

The key to your dreams is often what you are believing.

Believing in yourself and your capabilities is key.

You can study every bit of motivational material ever made, but if you don't believe in yourself, you can not be successful.

Self belief and self motivation are far stronger than the push of what we can learn from the outside.

Let the outside information light the fire as it is intended, be a keen learner of what is relevant, and motivate yourself by concentrating on what is important to you.

Motivate yourself , health, happiness and wealth.

Its possible for you now.

If you believe and push to achieve.

Chapter 2:

5 Habits of Bill Gates

Bill gates is a name synonymous with success. Who does not know Bill Gates? His footprints are everywhere. Students in elementary school look up to him as their role model. Those in high school and higher levels of education idolize him. He is a semi-god, everyone wanting to identify himself or herself with his success.

Well, here are 5 habits of Bill Gates:

1. He Is Generous

The 65-year-old founder of Microsoft Corporation is by no means a mean person (pun intended). He has donated to charity drives uncountable times. Many students are beneficiaries of his generosity through the Bill & Melinda Gates Foundation. He has come out strongly to support the education of black and Latino students, and those experiencing poverty in the United States.

Bill Gates – co-chair and trustee of Bill & Melinda Gates Foundation – has committed over $1.75 billion over two years for Covid-19 pandemic relief. He, besides Mackenzie Scott, Warren Buffet, and George Soros are among the wealthiest most generous people.

He understands perfectly that to him who much is given, much will be expected. The world is full of praises for the generosity of the world's fourth-richest person. His foundation is the world's largest charitable foundation and he has not stopped at that. To the father of three, poverty eradication is one of his life-long goals.

We can take a cue from him and start giving to receive. We should not always be the recipients of charities. Learn to give, not out of abundance but out of the love for humanity.

2. He Treasures His Family

It is an open secret that the father of three is a family man. It is amazing how he has been able to keep his family together all those years despite his wealth. Until May 4th 2021, Bill was married to Melinda. In a statement sent to the BBC, they said it was regrettable that they had to end their 27-year-old marriage. Nevertheless, his contribution to keeping his family close to his chest cannot be ignored.

He has not allowed his family affairs to come out to the public. Even when he divorced his wife in May 2021, they issued a joint statement to the media and kept their divorce under wraps. This is unlike the noisy and messy divorces that most celebrities have.

We learn from Bill Gates the importance of family. It is always God first and family next. Treasure your family because blood is always thicker than water. Whenever there is conflict, do not let it spill out to the public but sort it out amicably.

3. He Is A Social Man

From public appearances in social functions to corporate events, Bill Gates does not shy away from the public. He takes his time to attend personally to matters that require his presence. He has learned not to build a fortress or isolate himself.

With the type of publicity he receives, a man of his stature would naturally want to lead a quiet life and focus primarily on his businesses. However, he has a strong online presence. Be it LinkedIn, Twitter, Instagram, or Facebook, he shares his thoughts fearlessly.

Moreover, the technology giant founder engages captains of industry in meaningful and fruitful conversations. He has embraced the human nature of socializing and talking to people. Likewise, we should follow in tow. We should not live in fortresses because we will be cut off from the outside world and that will be the beginning of our downfall.

Attend that lunch or dinner with your colleagues, go to the graduation party of your associates, attend birthday parties and weddings. It is these social events and more that will link you with potential destiny connectors and you will grow your network. Your network is your net worth.

4. He Is Conscious of His Public Image

Bill Gates has created for himself an image of a calm and composed leader. Dressed in smart elegant suits for every occasion, the multi-billionaire never fails to impress. Not once can you fault the man over his dress code. Have you ever heard of the saying "dress how you want to be addressed?"

Your dressing speaks volumes as to the kind of person you are. Dressing in itself is an art. Carefully observe not to underdress or overdress because it sends an unspoken message to those you meet.

Never has the 65-year-old billionaire been involved in a public saga. He is careful to carry himself with decorum whenever he is in public. Public perception is key to maintain his social stature – an art he has perfected over the years. Even the speech he gives is in tandem with his public image.

The thought that Bill Gates can speak rumors or even argue in public is unfathomable. He is a towering icon of success and is careful not to belittle his image. It takes a lifetime to build a reputation but a few minutes to ruin it completely.

5. He Has A Progressive Mindset

It all begins from the mind. Our mindset is what makes us stand out. It is easier for Bill Gates to be content with what he has achieved so far. He made history as the youngest American billionaire at 31 years until Zuckerberg broke that record in 2010.

He has received numerous accolades and awards for his work, but he is still not content at that level. This does not mean that Bill is ungrateful. He is grateful. It is only that he has set his mind on much higher targets. That is the progressive mindset all of us ought to emulate.

Most people fall into the trap of settling down for less in the name of being altruistic. It is time to stop getting comfortable and borrow a page from the lifestyle of Bill. The mind is where reason is born. Bill

Gates knows this perfectly well and despite his wealth and achievements, he keeps moving forward.

Bill's progressive mindset has made him grow his corporation to become the world's biggest company with a valuation of $1 trillion. It begins and ends with the mind.

The above are 5 habits of Bill Gates that he has developed over time. They have made him who he is today.

Chapter 3:

7 Habits That Will Make You Successful

A man's habits are as good as his lifestyle. Some habits are akin to successful people. The path to greatness is less traveled and the habits to success may be difficult for some people to sustain.

The road to success is narrow and occasionally thorny because habits that will make you successful are uncomfortable and difficult to adapt. Similar to Charles Darwin's theory of survival for the fittest, only those who manage to trim their excesses and shape their habits will eventually be successful.

Here are seven habits that will make you successful:

1. <u>Integrity</u>

Integrity is one of the measures of success. It is the ability to live an honest life free from swindling, blackmail, and corruption among other vices. Integrity is the morality of a person and is relative from one person to another. However, there is a generally accepted threshold of integrity expected of people in different social, political, and economic classes.

Integrity is uncommon to most people making it highly valuable. People will forget how you looked but will never forget how you made them feel. Integrity holds back one from committing such awful mistakes. It will help you award the deserving, condemn vices, be intolerable to corruption, and make transparency your middle name.

The lack of integrity is responsible for the downfall of great people and business empires. Political leaders worldwide have lost their crown of glory to corruption. They were once the dream of every pupil in school and aspiring young leaders looked up to them. Corruption and greed stole that from them.

So powerful is integrity that successful people guard theirs' tooth and nail. Once eroded, their success is at stake. It may crumble down like a mound hill. Do you want to be successful? Have integrity.

2. <u>An Open Mind</u>

It is the ability to tolerate and be receptive to divergent ideas different from your beliefs. It takes a lot to accommodate the opinions of others and accept their reasoning to be rational. Successful people fully understand that they do not have a monopoly on brilliant ideas. As such, they cautiously welcome the proposals of other people while allowing room for further advancement.

Entertaining the ideas of other people does not mean blindly accepting them. It is the habit of successful people to be critical of everything, balancing their options and only settling for the best. An open mind translates to an analytical and inquisitive nature. The zeal to venture into the unknown and experiment with new waters.

Successful people are distinguished from others because they challenge the status quo. They seek to improve their best and develop alternatives to the existing routines. The reason why they are successful in the first place is their open mind.

How does one have an open mind? It is by being open to infinite possibilities of a hundred and one ways of approaching issues. Routine is an enemy of open-mindedness and by extension, success. It is of course inevitable not to follow a routine at our places of work, schools, or families. It is acceptable to that extent. Being its slave is completely unacceptable.

3. Move With Time

Time is never stagnant. The world evolves around time and seasons. The wise is he who deciphers and interprets them correctly. The measure of success in these modern times is different from those in the ancient days. A lot has changed.

In this era of technological advancements, we cannot afford to live in analog ways. The poor readers of seasons are stagnant in one position for a long time. Success is elusive in their hands. A look at business giants will reveal their mastery of times and seasons. They do not fumble at it. Not one bit.

Successful businesses deal with tools of the trade of the modern world. From the great Microsoft corporation to the Coca-cola company. All of them align themselves with the market demand presently. Learning the present time and season is a habit that will elevate you to success.

4. Learn From The Mistakes of Others

It is prudent to learn from the mistakes of other people and not from yours. Keenly observe those ahead of you and watch out not to fall into their traps. It is regretful to be unable to take a cue from our predecessors and learn from their failures.

Successful people travel down roads once taken (for the advantage of hindsight) by others – except for a few adventurous ones who venture into the unknown. The benefit of hindsight is very important because we learn from the mistakes of those who preceded us and adjust accordingly. Develop a habit of watching closely those ahead of you and take a cue from them not to commit similar mistakes. This habit will propel you to the doorstep of success.

5. Investment Culture

It is prudent to be mindful of tomorrow. No amount of investment is too little. Successful people do not consume everything they produce. They save a portion of their income for the future. Investment is a culture developed over time. Some people find it difficult to postpone the entire consumption of their income. They will only settle when nothing is left. This is retrogressive.

An investment culture curbs wastage and emphasizes tomorrow's welfare. Moreover, to reduce risk, the investment portfolio is diversified. It is dangerous to risk everything in one endeavor. Captains of industries worldwide have invested broadly in different sectors. This makes them stay afloat even during tough economic seasons.

6. Choosing Your Battles

On your way to success, do not make many enemies. This habit is ancient but very relevant to date. Unnecessary fights will wear you out and divert you away from the goal. Petty distractions will hijack your focus and successfully make you unsuccessful.

Learn to train your guns on things that matter. Feed your focus and starve your fears. Ignore useless petty issues that may lead to tainting of your public image. Fight your battles wisely.

7. Learn To Listen

Listening is an art beyond hearing. It is paying detailed attention to the speech of others, both verbal and non-verbal. Always listen more and talk less – a common argument for having two ears and one mouth. To be successful, you will have to pay closer attention to what is unspoken. Listen to the way people communicate. You will pick up genuine intentions in their speech and align yourself accordingly.

Once perfected, these seven habits will make you successful.

Chapter 4:

10 Habits to Change Your Life

I'm sure everyone wonders at a certain point in their life that what is the thing that is stopping them from reaching their goals. It is your bad and unhealthy habits that hold you down. If you want to succeed in life, you need to get rid of these habits and adopt healthy habits to help you in the long run.

Here are 10 healthy habits that will change your life completely if you can adopt them in your daily life:

1. Start Following a Morning Ritual

Everyone has something that they love to do, i.e., things that boost their energy and uplifts their mood. Find one for yourself and do that every morning. It will help you kickstart your day with a bright and cheerful mood. It will also help you to eliminate mental fatigue and stress. You will find yourself super energetic and productive. Let me tell you some morning rituals that you can try and get benefitted from.

- *Eating Healthy:* If you are very passionate about health and fitness, eating healthy as a morning ritual might be a win-win situation for you. You can have a nutritious breakfast every morning. Balance your breakfast with proper amounts of carbs, fats, proteins, etc. It will not only help you in staying healthy but will also help you kickstart your day on a proactive note.

- *Meditating:* Meditation is an excellent way of clearing your mind, enhancing your awareness, and improving your focus. You can meditate for 20 to 30 minutes every morning. Then you can take a nice warm shower, followed by a fresh cup of coffee. Most importantly, meditating regularly will also help you strengthen your immune system, promote emotional stability, and reduce stress.

- *Motivating:* A daily dose of motivation can work wonders for you. When you are motivated, your productivity doubles, and you make the best out of your day. Every morning, you can simply ask yourself questions like, "If it is the last day of your life, what do you want to do?", "What productive thing can I do today to make the best out of the day" "What do I need to do in order to avoid regretting later for having wasted a day?". When you ask yourself questions like these, you are actually instructing your brain to be prepared for having a packed-up and productive day.

- *Writing:* Writing can be a super-effective way of kickstarting your day. When you journal all your thoughts and emotions every day after waking up, it allows you to relieve yourself from all the mental clutter, unlocks your creative side, and sharpens your focus.

- *Working Out:* Working out is a great morning ritual that you can follow every day. When you work out daily, it helps you burn more fat, improves your blood circulation, and boosts your energy level. If you are interested in fitness and health, this is the perfect morning ritual for you. You can do some cardio exercises, or some strength training, or both. Depending on your suitability, create a workout routine for yourself and make sure to stick to that. If you don't stick to your routine, it won't be of much help.

2. Start Following the 80/20 Rule

The 80/20 rule states that almost 20% of the tasks you perform are responsible for yielding 80% of the results. It is why you should invest more time in tasks that can give you more significant results instead of wasting your time on tasks that yield little to no results. In this way, you can not only save time but also maximize your productivity. Most importantly, when you see the results after performing those tasks, you will be more motivated to complete the following tasks. After you have finished performing these tasks, now you can quickly move your concentration and focus towards other activities that you need to do throughout your day.

3. Practice Lots of Reading

Reading is a great habit and a great way to stimulate your creativity and gaining more knowledge. When you get immersed in reading, it calms you and improves your focus, almost similar to meditating. If you practice reading before going to bed, you are going to have a fantastic sleep. You can read non-fiction books, which will help you seek motivation, develop new ideas, and broaden your horizon. You can also get a lot of advice about how to handle certain situations in life.

4. Start Single-tasking

Multitasking is hard, and almost 2% of the world's total population can do this properly. You can try multitasking occasionally. If you keep on trying to do this all the time, it will form a mental clutter, and as a result, your brain won't be able to filter out unnecessary information. Many studies have suggested that it can severely damage your cognitive control and lower your efficiency when you multitask a lot. It is the main reason why you should try to do single-tasking more than multitasking. Prepare a list of all the tasks you need to perform in a day and start with the most important one. Make sure not to rush and to complete one thing at a time.

5. Start Appreciating More

Appreciating things is totally dependent on your mentality. For example, some people can whine and complain about a glass being half empty, whereas some people appreciate that there is half a glass of water. It totally depends on your point of view and way of thinking. People get blinded by the urge to reach success so much that they actually forget to appreciate the little things in life. If you are working and earning a handsome salary, don't just sit and complain about why you are not earning more, what you need to do to achieve that, etc. You should obviously aim high, but not at the cost of your well-being. When you practice gratitude, it increases your creativity, improves your physical health, and reduces your stress. You can start writing about the things you are grateful for in your journal every day before going to bed, make some time for appreciating your loved ones, or remind yourself of all the things you are grateful for before going to bed every day. If you are not happy with your current situation, you will not be happy in the future. You need to be happy and satisfied at first, and then only you can work on progressing further.

6. Always Keep Positive People Around You

When you have toxic people around you, it gets tough for you to stay in a good mood or achieve something good in life. Toxic people always find a way to pull you down and make you feel bad about yourself. You should always surround yourself with people who are encouraging and positive. When you do that, your life is going to be full of positivity.

7. Exercise on a Regular Basis

Start exercising regularly to maintain good health and enhancing your creativity and cognitive skills. It also increases your endurance level and boosts your energy. When you exercise regularly, your body produces more endorphins. These hormones work as anti-depressants.

8. Start Listening More

Effective communication is very important in maintaining both professional and personal relationships. For communicating effectively, you need to work on your listening capability first. You need to pay attention to the things said by others instead of focusing only on what you have to say. Listening to others will allow you to understand them better. When you listen to someone, it makes them understand that they are valued and that you are here to listen to them. When they feel important and valued, they also start paying attention to what you say, thereby contributing to effective communication. Don't try to show fake concentration while you are busy thinking about something else. When you listen more, you learn more.

9. Take a Break from Social Media (Social Media Detox)

Many studies have shown that excessive use of social media can contribute to depression. Most importantly, it wastes a lot of time because people meaninglessly scroll, swipe, and click for hours. It is a very unhealthy habit and is very bad for bothe physical and mental health. Sometimes you need to completely stop using social media for a while to reduce mental clutter and stress. Turn off your laptops and phones every day for a few hours. It will help you to reconnect with the surrounding world and will uplift your mood.

10. Start Investing More in Self-care

Make some time for yourself out of your busy schedule. It is going to boost your self-esteem, improve your mental health, and uplift your mood. You need to do at least one thing for yourself every day that will make you feel pampered and happy. You can prepare a mouth-watering meal, take a comfortable bubble bath, learn something new, or just relax while listening to music.

The moment you start introducing these habits in your daily, you will instantly see change. Remember that even a tiny step towards a positive change can give outstanding results if you stay consistent.

Chapter 5:

10 Habits Maria Sharapova

Maria Sharapova, a Russian tennis player, has elevated to victory and recognition on the tennis court since 2004. She started her training at Nick Bollettieri's tennis program at the age of seven. By the age of 11, she had signed a contract with Nike and had won three grand slams in ten years.

Sharapova has achieved a great deal of success due to her drive, including being ranked world No. 1 in singles, and she is also the only Russian with a career in Grand Slam. Her focus and perseverance in the face of adversity are what made her such a formidable opponent on the court. Here are 10 Maria Sharapova habits that might intrigue you.

1. She Keeps It Real

After being barred from competing in tennis after failing a drug test, many expected Sharapova to retire. But she was unfazed by the attention, returned to the court and continued playing the sport of her dreams. People will expect different things from you, but the essential value is being loyal to yourself. Pay attention to your vision and enthusiasm, and then keep going.

2. She Is Open to Other Opportunities

As a successful athlete, many possibilities with high potential will land right to you. The majority comes from sponsorships, endorsements, and even modelling. Maria has had her fair share of opportunities like modelling, advertising for Nike, Prince, Canon, and Cole Haan.

3. She Respects Her Body

On February 26th, 2020, Sharapova abruptly declared her retirement from tennis. News which took aback her admirers, other athletes, and, of course, the media.

Her reasons for retiring included several injuries-shoulder injuries that had lasted her entire career, a back problem, and a thigh injury that were beginning to impact her health. Furthermore, she had to learn to listen to her body and respect its boundaries.

4. She Focuses on What She Can Control

Sharapova stated during a sports conference that she has always controlled what she could, which is how to go out there, compete, and manage her career time, and how she used to play tennis. Relax and let life take its course where you can't control.

5. She Lives and Works on Her Terms

When Sharapova's was barred from playing, the penalty might have effectively terminated her career as a tennis champion. However, she did not allow this to happen.

After all, adversity might strike at any time. Similar to Sharapova case, when this happens, it's becomes metaphorical and side-line you. That is why she believes in the importance of being strong and making every moment matter.

6. She Consciously Does What She Loves

Sharapova stated at a sports conference that it is ideal never to take an opportunity for granted. Working and leading with a moral conscience is vital when you love what you do and doing it with passion and integrity. Know who you are and what you stand for.

7. She Adores Her Idols

Monica Seles was one of Sharapova's childhood idols. She admired her tenacity and focus on the court while playing. The admiration of her Idols, as she noted, strengthened her urge and determination always to win and be her competitive self. Having an idol in your athlete path or any other life prospect can lead you to a more incredible deal.

8. Worrying Is Not Her Thing

Sharapova is a fan of what she does without giving regard to her opponents. She competed with older and more powerful players, which helped her improve and prepared her to compete against players of her calibre. She was never interested in who other players are and the tournaments they competed in. Worrying too much can do you more harm than better hence you should not be concerned about what your opponent is doing.

9. She Focuses on Making It Better

Sharapova's desire to win always helped her focus on the court during tournaments. She considered herself as a "tough guy" who didn't like losing at all. When you put in the work, it can appear excruciatingly tricky, but you never know when that will pay off.

10. She Enjoys Reading

Sharapova unwinds after a long day by reading. She enjoys reading a lot. She revealed that reading serves her meditation and works on your creativity.

Conclusion

Two things separate the good from the great. First, you don't have to play tennis to learn from Sharapova. All in all, her confidence, and focus even under pressure, brings a glimpse of life while facing challenges.

Chapter 6:

Meditate For Focus

Meditation calms the mind and helps you to focus on what is important. It dims the noise and brings your goals into clearer vision.

Meditation has been practised as far back as 5000bc in India - with meditation depicted in wall artisan from that period.
That is 1500 years older than any written artefact ever found.
It is as old as the archaeological evidence of any human society.

Meditation can change the structure of the brain promoting focus, learning and better memory, as well as lowering stress and reducing the chances of anxiety and depression.

Whilst there are many different types and ways to meditate,
the ultimate goal is to clear your mind and calm your body
so that you can focus on your dream.
Aim to look inward for answers.
It could be aided by music relating to your dream or videos.
The music, the images, and imagining you are already living that life will bring it into reality.

Your mind creates the vision and the feeling
in your heart will bring it to you.
When your mind and heart work together it creates balance,
leading to happiness and success.

Meditation is the process of bringing the

visions of the mind and the desires of the heart together,

which in turn will form your life.

Meditation clears all the threats to this -

such as worry and distraction.

It will bring you clear focus and open up the next steps in your journey.

Meditation is often best done when you first wake or before you go to

sleep, but it can be incorporated into your day.

If clear consistent thought brings decisive action and success,

it is important to dwell on your dreams as often as possible.

Calm your mind of the unnecessary noise that is robbing you of your

focus.

The more realistic you make this vision

and the more you feel it in your heart,

the quicker it will come.

Meditation can help you achieve this

whether you follow a guide or make it up yourself.

The key is calm and focus.

Your subconscious knows how to get there.

Meditation will help open up that knowledge.

Science is just beginning to unlock the answers on why meditation is so effective, even so it has been used for over 7000 years to help people relax and focus on their goals.

The positive health and well-being evidence of meditation is well documented.

We may not yet understand it fully,

But just know that it works and use it every day.

You don't need to understand every detail to use something that works.

Meditation is perhaps one of the most time tested tools in existence.

It could work for you, if you try it.

It could change your life forever.

Chapter 7:

10 Habits of Michael Phelps

With 28 medals, 23 of which are gold, Michael Phelps is the greatest and most decorated Olympian in history. His career included five Olympic Games and two decades of supremacy. Even though Phelps competes in a sport where exceptionally talented athletes can win gold medals over various distances and strokes, his achievements dwarf those of any other athletes.

His competitive nature and a strong desire to always win have everything to do with his breakthrough. How did Phelps become the world's most excellent swimmer?

Here are the ten habits of Michael Phelps.

1. Dream Big and Set Outlandish Goals

According to Phelps, "the more you dream, and your goals, the more you achieve greatness." He desired a swimming career and had goals of becoming the best. He had to put in a lot of effort to attain his ambitions, including earning a gold medal at the Olympic Games. You won't achieve anything unless you dream big and set lofty aspirations.

2. Dare Doing New Things

Nothing is impossible, according to Phelps, as long as you are willing to try it out. Phelps understands how tough it is to win an Olympic gold medal, but he was motivated to do it and make history. Don't step back from trying new things because you are not sure of the outcomes.

3. Believe That Anything Is Possible

Phelps was able to become the finest swimmer in the world because he believed in himself. He also believes that God answers prayers of those who have faith and strive hard to achieve their goals. You must believe that anything is possible as you strive to achieve it.

4. Utilize Both Your Strengths and Weaknesses

Michael Phelps is well-known for his athleticism. His workouts are tough, and has best genetic attributes. However, he has ADHD and uses it as fuel for his swimming. Just like Phelps, your strengths and weaknesses are your biggest motivation.

5. Maintain Strict Self-Control

There is no quick way to greatness. You must put in the effort if you want to be successful at anything. For Phelps to be a world-class athlete, you must sustain world-class actions. He trains for 6 hours a day, seven days a week. When he is not doing physical training, he rests, allowing his muscles to relax while meditating and visualizing.

6. Don't Give Up

Michael Phelps is a real example of how you shouldn't allow your failures define or ruin you. Just triumph over them no matter what. Remember how Phelps' reputation was tarnished after he was detained from his drunk and drinking habits? Despite the anguish, he always came back strong.

7. Get a Puppy

Phelps has a dog named Herman, a bulldog he adores and makes him more responsible. Moreover, it helps him in managing his ADHD. Having a pet makes you more accountable, empathic, compassionate, and disciplined.

8. Give It Your Best

Phelps physical traits-his hands and feet can function as paddles, and his height form glides effortlessly through the water. For sure, he was a swimmer! Michael learned of his exceptional talent and persisted in becoming an Olympic champion. It would be great if you always practiced what you are best at to excel in it.

9. Survive the Odds for Success

When his career was setting off, Phelps achieved zero notable positions. He lost in several championships, which crushed him as a young swimmer. He did not, however, quit. He trained harder than ever before, and in the 2008 Beijing Olympics, he won eight gold medals, breaking the record for the most gold medals won in a single sport. Hung in there, despite the setbacks, persevere, and eventually, you'll triumph.

10. Be Self-Assured Enough To Declare Your Aspirations

There was no doubt that Michael was born to be a legend, and he was not afraid to let the world know about it. His pride in letting people know his plans to win several gold medals was constantly chastised as arrogance, but his fans always had his back. Yes, there will be sceptics, but letting your friends and family in to a portion of your goals keep you motivated.

Conclusion

There is doubt that Michael Phelps is an excellent swimmer and a champion given that he has set and broken several world records. Just like Phelps, your career, personal life, and other areas of your life will be defined by your daily routine. His habits are definitely a 100% worth of mentoring you towards being the best you can be.

Chapter 8:

How To Stop Wasting Time

In the inspiring words of Marcia Wider, "It's how we spend our time here, and now, that really matters. If you are fed up with the way you have come to interact with time, change it."

Indeed, time waits for no man. The ticking of the clock should be a startling revelation to you that how precious our time on this earth is. A study conducted at the University of Calgary shows that the ratio of chronic procrastination has increased from 5% in 1978 to 26% in 2007. In other words, you don't need more time. You have to do MORE with the time you already have. Stop wasting your time on the things that don't really matter. Do you realize how many seconds and minutes and hours do we waste every day on stuff that doesn't even let us come close to reaching our goals? If you've ever come to ask yourself, "where does the time go?" then maybe you should re-think how and on what you're spending your time.

"A man who dares to waste one hour has not discovered the value of time." Charles Darwin. There are only as many as 24 hours in a day, and you've got to make sure that each of them counts for something. There's a date on the left side of the tombstone, that's the date on which you were born. When you die, another date is engraved on the right side of your tombstone, but that dash, that line that you see in the middle of both these dates, decides how much you left your mark on other people's lives as well as your own, how much you were able to impact others, that dash represents how you lived your life in the timeframe that you were given.

We all get the same amount of time. A homeless person or a beggar that wanders here and there all day brings the same amount of time as the most successful businessman. It's what we do with that time, how we presume the ticking of the clock that genuinely matters. Life flickers by us in the blink of an eye. And what do we do about that? We only give excuses and justifications. "I don't have time to go to the gym, and maybe I'll start tomorrow. I'll start studying tomorrow; one day of taking a break won't make a difference" NO! It would make all the difference in the world. Stop fearing and pitying yourself and get up. Stop wasting your time because it's a depreciating asset, and you won't get any of it back.

You have to take the first step. You can't just live your life fearing the challenges and efforts you have to put in to get somewhere higher in life. Procrastinating, watching your favorite TV show adds up to so much time, even for an hour each day. And that time is nothing but wasted. Imagine the knowledge you can gain in that one hour of each day, imagine the work that you could do, the language that you can learn, the instrument that you can learn to play. So start investing your time into something productive rather than just lying here making defenses.

"Newton's first law of productivity" states that objects at rest tend to stay at rest until they're acted upon. That book on your shelf isn't going to read itself, those weights in the gym aren't going to move by themselves, that long due essay isn't going to write itself, YOU. HAVE. TO. DO. IT! And you have to do it now. Don't wait for another hour or another day or another week; you have to take that leap of faith; you have to take that risk. Specify your days, prioritize your to-do list, eliminate all the distractions. Nothing will make you happier than knowing that you're making progress towards becoming a better version of yourself. Take breaks, but get yourself back up to your goals. Don't waste your time! "Whatever you want to do, do it now! There are only so many tomorrow's." – Pope Paul VI.

FOCUS! You should be terrified of living a life on the sidelines. Of not achieving anything whether you're 6, 16, or 60. Of doing nothing and watching the time passes by, of not making any progress and not being able to come closer to your dreams, your goals. Stop being stagnant! Start working towards your passion, your dreams, your aspirations. The separator between the people that win and lose is what we do with that time, with those seconds that we get in a day. Start working towards self-mastery, and you will begin to see the difference in all the dimensions of your life. So concentrate on developing yourself because if you don't, I guarantee you that you will make a settlement, and most people have, and most of us already have. The proper function of a man is to live, not just only to exist. We shall not waste our days trying to prolong them only, but we shall use our time effectively.

Time is free, but it's also priceless. It's perhaps the most essential commodity in this world. Once you've lost it, you can never get it back. Look back and see how many hours and days and years have you wasted doing absolutely nothing? Don't shy up from the tough things. We can't make excuses and then expect to be successful at the same time. We have to get up every day and make sure we don't quit ourselves, our goals, our dreams, our passions. Make mistakes, make them thousand times over, but make sure you learn something from every single one of them. We can't travel back to time and change the past. So don't dwell on the things that happened yesterday or months ago. Start working towards your future. We only have a limited time here on earth. It's better to spend time waiting for the opportunity to take action than miss the chance.

"Determine never to be idle. No person will have occasion to complain of the want of time who never loses any. It is wonderful how much can be done if we are always doing." - Thomas Jefferson.

Chapter 9:

How To Reprogram
Your Mind For Success

Your routines are the things that drive you through life. Your routines are driven by your emotions. Your emotions are a sum of your past. Your past is a sum of incidents. These incidents may be related to a person or a thing, which in turn make your life exciting.

You start your day with a thought. A thought that wakes you up every day. A unique thought that everyone experiences every morning. These thoughts are the driving force for you to get up whether you like it or not.

These thoughts may be fear-driven or love memories. So your brain creates emotions in your subconscious mind which in turn dictates your daily tasks and routine.

You might be having doubts about a leave from a job that you might deserve because you can't get the doubt of getting fired out of your mind.

You might be remembering a loved one that you want to see today.

You may be hoping to get some good news today.

So you have a set routine every day, that you follow without even ever pondering on day-to-day life. And this is the ultimate failure of your purpose in life.

A routine that is not getting you forward in life isn't worth living with. But you are not able to think about it because your mind and your subconscious have taken over your body.

As all these obvious things are being stated, close your eyes, put some music on, shut the doors or sit on a bench in a quiet part. Tell your mind to get rid of those memories that drive your emotions. Leave your body motionless and try to take deep breaths.

As you start doing this, you will feel an immediate thought kick in your subconscious. Your mind will be making you feel like something is missing or if you had something to do.

This is an uncomfortable state of mind. But now is your time to be your own master. Tell your subconscious that it is your will that leads you, but not the emotions and your mind.

You have to realize the reality and make it seem more acceptable to your brain. You have to make it feel confident and feel that it is helping you to stay commited in any situation that comes across in your life.

You need to become conscious in this hectic world of involuntary unconsciousness.

You have to make yourself ready for the unpredictable future. Because if you are not ready for the future, you are still drowning in your past.

Everyone's past is toxic. Even good memories can be toxic. One might ask how.

The memories of the past either make your stay in the bed or they make you hope full of chances to come with luck. But luck is rarely lucky.

You cannot be a free man till you dive out of your personal reality that your brain has created to keep you in your comfort zone. You cannot become successful if you stay on your laptop or your phone interacting with the world via social media and emails.

You have to create your own environment by making new friends, taking new jobs, asking questions to your partner, making a change in your natural habitat.

Your mind is the curator of your environment and the people in it. So you have to change your environment by making your mind commit to your orders.

Give your mind a free space to rehabilitate and renew itself. Give it a chance to imagine new things. Make it wander off like a herd of cattle in the grasslands. Let it flow without any emotion, just to create enough space for new realities to pop in. As soon as it does, you will f

Tiny Habits

PART 3

Chapter 1:

Five Habits We Consider

Harmless

Familiarity breeds contempt. There are habits that we have become so accustomed to that hinder us from achieving our full potential. We consider them little and insignificant in our lives. Sometimes, we go to the extremes of defending ourselves when we are corrected and advised to abandon them. It is a sad state to be in and one that requires enlightenment and self-awareness to be able to get out of that quagmire. Here are five habits that we consider harmless:

1. Blue Screen Addiction

Blue screen addiction is the addiction to digital media and video games. This is a common problem, especially for millennials. It is often considered inconsequential, a myth that has been debunked by real-life experiences.

Most people spend a lot of time working through their computers, using their mobile phones or tablets, playing video games, or watching television. The use of digital media in this era is almost unavoidable. Regardless of this digital evolution, there have been some excesses. Heavy use of these devices has broken the social code since most people can only communicate through communication apps and not physically.

Faceless cyberbullies have attacked and trolled innocent netizens and ruined their reputation.

News spread fast via the internet and it is not a surprise that addiction to blue screens is on the rise. It is not as harmless as it may seem and its effects are long-lasting. It causes poor eyesight and sometimes migraines.

2.   Procrastination

It is the habit of postponing tasks to be done presently to a later time. Most people relate to this habit that has grown roots in our lifestyle. Before you judge yourself harshly for doing this, statistics have it that over 80% of college students engage in procrastination and it has chronically affected at least 20% of adults. That is just the tip of the iceberg.

We comfort ourselves that we are not alone in this ocean that has drowned the ambitions and potential of many people. We err in finding comfort in this well-dressed misery of procrastination. It is not as harmless as it superficially looks.

Procrastination encourages laziness which has, in turn, made many people pay a higher price for engaging in it. Some have lost their employment for leaving incomplete tasks at work, others have missed out on promotions for incompetence and a further group has failed to secure business opportunities that required their attention at the opportune time when they had put everything on hold. What is the cost we are ready to pay for in procrastination?

We should sober up and abandon procrastination by acting on matters that need our immediate attention. Shelving our response for a later time causes more harm than good.

3. Making Obnoxious Jokes

There is a limit to the extreme one can go when making jokes. It should never go overboard to hurt the feelings of our friends and associates. Many times we underestimate or maybe do not consider the impact our words may have on our friends and those around us. We unknowingly hurt their self-esteem and they feel worthless after what turns out to be a bad joke. We should always know when to stop and apologize for our excesses because we never know how much we have hurt our friends when we make bad jokes about them.

It is inconsiderate of us not to take into account the struggles of our friends when we make fun of their situation. It seems harmless but has the potential to completely cut off one's dreams.

4. Building A Fortress

The single greatest mistake that we unknowingly commit is building a fortress for ourselves to hide from the rest of the world. Indeed, the world can sometimes be cruel and unforgiving, making us run to the nearest point of safety. We build walls instead of bridges to separate us from the harsh reality. This solution is short-lived because the fortress will cut you off from the rest of the world.

You will live in solitude without any news and over time your resources will be depleted. The fortress may not necessarily be physical but also social. As much as introverts manage to keep off squabbles and fights, they lack a network to connect. It is not safe to be alone in this ever-changing world. Find a person or group with whom you share common interests and build a network.

Your network is your net worth.

5. Glossing Over Facts

Facts should be the language you speak. We often omit or ignore facts that we deem irrelevant to us but surprisingly turn out to be very important. When you get your facts right, everything falls into place. Often, the average person does not go into the details. Remember the devil lies in the details? It is therein where you will find solutions to matters that you overlooked.

Stand out by grasping correct facts about a matter before you indulge in them. It is harmful not to be aware of your surroundings or get your facts right because it puts your competence on the relevant subject matter in question.

You should check out these five habits that we mistakenly consider harmless and adjust your approach.

Chapter 2:

10 Habits of Mark Zuckerberg

Few entrepreneurs can claim to have radically impacted digital communication, but Mark Zuckerberg can. Zuckerberg is one of the well-known personalities whose shared experiences will teach you the true meaning of success.

He invented Facebook from his Harvard dorm room, which would eventually revolutionize and, in some ways, create social media. Zuckerberg has demonstrated an ability to adapt to changing circumstances, which is crucial in the volatile digital field. Despite the company's ups and downs, controversies and upsets, Zuckerberg drives from the helm while securing the genius he founded.

Following the successful path of Mark Zuckerberg, discipline and purposeful life and work balance are key. Here are ten habits that Zuckerberg swears to have enabled his success.

1. Simplicity

Mark Zuckerberg's all-time quote, "Make things as simple as possible, but not simpler", has certainly lauded a spot in his invention. With Facebook, he made it super simple, focusing on must-have items-with simple features like "likes, friends, events."

Bare-bones, right? Understanding and practising this underlying principle can land your brand market-friendly. Make your brand simple!

2. Your "No" Is a Huge No

On several occasions, Zuckerberg received massive buyout bids, there were numerous proposals, such as new product features or collaborations. But he always stuck to his objective-if anything didn't fit, he'd say "no."

Your imaginative focus-whether it's your job, business, or innovation, must be exceptionally strong. Distractions from little concerns can be fatal, especially for startups.

3. Your Mission

Mark Zuckerberg's aim to connect the globe drew skilled engineers and financiers, who assisted him in creating an easily understandable platform. If you don't know your mission, how will you be able to lead the charge? How will your employees or customers know? The importance of a clear-cut mission cannot be overlooked. Make your task precise and clear.

4. Learning Is Continuous

Developing personal goals is a powerful, unequaled technique to boost your cognitive abilities, cultivate self-reliance, and boost your creativity. Zuckerberg spends more than 50 hours each week overseeing his businesses.

However, he does not devote all of his brainpower to his 9-5 job, so he reads to develop his cognitive ability. Just as Zuckerberg, enhancing your path means you're up to reading habit. Knowledge is power!

5. Equanimity

This is indeed a fancy way of showing that when Zuck is under pressure or in a stressful circumstance, he does not lose his cool. Instead, he confronts even the most difficult challenges calmly since anger doesn't really breed success; it only serves to alienate an impression that you lack control over a situation. Developing this stability will help you improve your relationships and critically enable you to deal with or work under pressure.

6. Self-confidence

Zuckerberg is not interested in being led or doing things on the basis of others. "Sometimes you're going to do unpopular stuff, and you're going to make mistakes," he said in an interview with Wired Magazine.
You must be willing to take chances. Such a mindset lends a distinct "make it" stride to your product, brand, or service. Worrying about how something will work will not lead to success; instead, you must get in and do it.

7. Heedfulness

Zuckerberg is unfazed by his critics. Your ability to ignore the noises around you will save your energy on focusing on the things that matter most.

Instead, channel that energy into creativity, invention, and behaviors that will help you succeed. It is vital that your conscious approach to what you want to accomplish blocks out all the external influences.

8. Rationality

Zuckerberg is always looking for ways to delve deeper into an issue or idea in order to make a difference, be disruptive, and maximize value. Success comes from critically evaluating your thoughts rather than simply accepting the first idea that comes to mind.

9. You're a Convergent-Thinker

Zuckerberg has always prioritized on solving problems. As he noted in a biography about him, he's always questioning any initiative that he partakes. At the heart of every industry you consider creating or doing, you are solving a relevant problem to help your target users or business.

10. Effective Communication

Unlike other leaders, Zuckerberg is always up to communicating with his team, giving them a chance to share their talent, regardless of rank, hence possibly achieving a more enlightened workplace. Maintaining open lines of communication with your team not only develops trust, but it can also help you be a more effective leader. When you establish a working atmosphere that emphasizes communication, it makes reasonable that Zuck would take this approach with his staff as well.

Conclusion

Maybe you'll fail. You'll waste valuable time and money on a dubious venture. People around you will tell you thousands of times, "I told you so." But, there's always the possibility that you'll succeed. If you don't try, you'll never know.

Chapter 3:

How To Rid Yourself of Distraction

Distraction and disaster sound rather similar.

It is a worldwide disorder that you are probably suffering from.

Distraction is robbing you of precious time during the day.

Distraction is robbing you of time that you should be working on your goals.

If you don't rid yourself of distraction, you are in big trouble.

It is a phenomenon that most employees are only productive 3 out of 8 hours at the office.

If you could half your distractions, you could double your productivity.

How far are you willing to go to combat distraction?

How badly do you want to achieve proper time management?

If you know you only have an hour a day to work, would it help keep you focused?

Always focus on your initial reason for doing work in the first place.

After all that reason is still there until you reach your goal.

Create a schedule for your day to keep you from getting distracted.

Distractions are everywhere.

It pops up on your phone.

It pops up from people wanting to chat at work.

It pops up in the form of personal problems.

Whatever it may be, distractions are abound.

The only cure is clear concentration.

To have clear concentration it must be something you are excited about.

To have clear knowledge that this action will lead you to something exciting.

If you find the work boring, It will be difficult for you to concentrate too long.
Sometimes it takes reassessing your life and admitting your work is boring for you to consider a change in direction.

Your goal will have more than one path.
Some paths boring, some paths dangerous, some paths redundant, and some paths magical.
You may not know better until you try.
After all the journey is everything.

If reaching your goal takes decades of work that makes you miserable, is it really worth it?
The changes to your personality may be irreversible.

Always keep the goal in mind whilst searching for an enjoyable path to attain it.
After all if you are easily distracted from your goal, then do you really want it?

Ask yourself the hard questions.
Is this something you really want? Or is this something society wants for you?

Many people who appear successful to society are secretly miserable.
Make sure you are aware of every little detail of your life.
Sit down and really decide what will make you happy at the end of your life.

What work will you be really happy to do?
What are the causes and people you would be happy to serve?
How much money you want?
What kind of relationships you want?
If you can build a clear vision of this life for you, distractions will become irrelevant.
Irrelevant because nothing will be able to distract you from your perfect vision.

Is what you are doing right now moving you towards that life?
If not stop, and start doing the things what will.
It really is that simple.

Anyone who is distracted for too long from the task in hand has no business doing that task. They should instead be doing something that makes them happy.

We can't be happy all the time otherwise we wouldn't be able to recognize it.
But distraction is a clear indicator you may not be on the right path for you.
Clearly define your path and distraction will be powerless.

Chapter 4:

10 Habits of Happy People

Happy people live the most satisfying lives on the planet. They have come to understand the importance of not worrying because it will not make any differential change in their lives. If you cannot control the outcome of a process, why worry? If you can control and make a difference to the outcome of a situation, why worry? Worrying does not bring an ounce of success your way.

Here are 10 habits of happy people that could be you if you choose to adopt it:

1. Happy People Count Their Blessings.

Taking stock of your successes is an important part of appreciating yourself. You find comfort in knowing that despite all the hiccups you have found in your journey there remains an oasis of achievements in your desert.

Everyone needs to take stock of what is in his or her basket of blessings. It is a reminder of your resilience and persistence in the face of challenges. It is an indication of your ability and a minute representation of the progress you can make, given time.

Remind yourself of the taste of victory in your small achievements. It begins with understanding that you definitely cannot be able to win it all. There are grey and shadow areas that will not be within your reach.

2. Happy People Do Not Need the Validation of Others.

Happy people do not wait for the validation of other people. They are autonomous. Develop the habit of doing what is right regardless of your audience and you will have an authentic lifestyle. As such, your source of happiness will be independent of uncontrollable factors. Why should you tie your happiness to someone else capable of ruining your day in a snap? This is not to mean that you will not need other people. Humans are social beings and interdependent. Letting them strongly influence your lifestyle is the major problem. Be your own man.

3. They Are Bold.

Boldly and cautiously pursuing their ambitions is part of the ingredients that make up happy people. Knowing what you want is one thing and pursuing it is another. If music is your passion and it makes you happy, chase after it for it is therein that your happiness lies. Whatever it is (of course considering its legality) do not let it pass.

To be truly happy, do not live in the shadow of other happy people. Define your happiness and drink from your well. Timidity will make you bask under the shade of giants and create a sense of false security. One day the shade will be no more and leave you exposed to an unimaginable reality.

4. They are social people.

Being social is one common characteristic of happy people. Happiness makes them bubbly and alive. There is a common testament in almost all happy people – either happiness made them social or their social nature made them happy. Thanks to whichever of the two came earlier, they are happy people!

Like bad luck, happiness is contagious. Your social circle can infect you with happiness or even deny it to you. Being sociable does not mean to the extreme nature with all the hype that comes along.

It means being approachable to people. Some will positively add to your basket and others will offer positive criticism towards your cause. With such input, your happiness will have longevity.

5. Believe in a greater cause.

Happy people understand that it is not always about them. There is a greater cause above their interests. They do not derive their happiness from the satisfaction of their needs and wants. Regardless of any deficiency in their lives, their flame of happiness is not easily put out.

Do you want to be happy? It is time to put self-interest aside and not tie your happiness to local anchors. An average person's happiness is mainly dependent on his well-being. Refusing to be average gives you leverage over those out to put off your happiness.

6. Lead a purposeful life.

Are there happy people without purpose? Those we see happy maintain their status by having a powerful drive towards the same. A strong purpose will make you stay on happiness' lane. It is the habit of happy people to have a purpose. This is to enable them to stay on course.

Being happy is not a permanent state. It is easily reversible if caution is not taken. Purposefulness is part of the caution taken by happy people.

7. Admit they are human.

To err is human. Given this, happy people appreciate the erroneous nature of man and accept the things they cannot change, have the courage to change the things they can, and the wisdom to know the difference. A prayer commonly referred to as the serenity prayer.
Admitting being human is the first step towards being happy. You forgive yourself of your wrongs before seeking the forgiveness of another. This brings inner peace culminating in happiness.

8. Know their strengths and weaknesses.

Being aware of your strengths and weaknesses is one thing happy people have mastered. Through that, they know their limits; the time to push and time to take a break. This serves to help avoid unwarranted disappointments that come along with new challenges.
Nothing can put off the charisma of a prepared spirit. Happy people know their limitations well enough such that no ill-willed voice can whisper disappointments to them. They hold the power of self-awareness within their hearts making them live with contentment.

9. Notice the contributions of those around them.

No man is an island. The contributions of other people in our lives cannot be emphasized enough. We are because they are (for all the good reasons). At any one point in our lives, someone made us happy. The first step is noticing the roles played by those in our immediate environment.

The joy of being surrounded by people to hold our hands in life is engraved deeper in our hearts in times of need. It is time you stop looking far away and turn your eyes to see what is next to you.

10. <u>They are grateful and appreciative.</u>

"Thank you" is a word that does not depart from the lips of happy people. Their hearts are trained to focus on what is at their disposal instead of what they cannot reach. It is crystal that a bird in hand is worth two in the bush.

Happy people continue being happy despite deficiencies. Try being appreciative and see how happiness will tow along.

Adopt these 10 habits of happy people and depression will keep away from you. If you want to be happy, do what happy people do and you will see the difference.

Chapter 5:

10 Habits of Serena Williams

Serena Williams is one of the greatest tennis players of all time. To win 23 grand slams, she had to overcome obstacles that most tennis players don't face: she is a black woman in a predominantly white sport, grew up in a poor neighbourhood that was not always safe, she endured intense scrutiny of her body, racism, and misogyny.

Despite this, she still manages to be an exceptional tennis player. Williams has epitomized the grit, resilience, and mental toughness required to overcome every obstacle and hardship she has had to endure since the beginning of her career, hence inspiring athletes worldwide.

Here are 10 habits of Serena Williams for your life lessons.

1. Make Your Path

Your path is unique to you and only you. Serena has never followed a script. She was raised in Compton, California, trained by her father, mostly eschewed the junior circuit-the traditional path to tennis success. Her emergence on the scene as a teenager player to embracing her physical prowess and chiselled figure says it all. She told Robin Roberts in an interview that she is only up to win, and inspire people.

2. Adapt Well

To maintain success, you must welcome change. Adaptability includes the ability to recover rapidly from adversity. Serena Williams demonstrates her adaptability by playing on the scorching hot hard court of the Australian Open, the slick clay of the rainy French Open, and the quick grass of Wimbledon. That implies that she delves deep when necessary.

3. Enjoy the Moment

When it comes to stressful situations, Serena enjoy seizing the opportunity to differentiate herself from the competition. Does she ever doubt herself? Yes! She accepts it, bottle it up, and toss the bottle away. Her mind-set is one that you can grasps.

4. Fuel a Work-Life Balance

Bring your entire being to everything you do. Serena's work-life balance is well-documented: she is a minority owner of the Miami Dolphins, makes her clothing and footwear, heads charity, and is a wife and mother. These outlets shape who she is as a person, and maintaining a healthy balance translates into complete focus and performance.

5. Fight Till the End

Serena has made it a point never to give up. She fights till the end in everything she does, and it has led to her incredible success. Nothing seems to break her! Coming from a poor upbringing, she has fought her way to the top. You may not be able to move or serve as she does, but you can always fight as she does.

6. Focus

Williams once stated, "if you can keep playing tennis when someone is shooting a gun down the street, that's focus!" Thanks to the tough times in her Compton upbringing, Serena has been focusing her way up to success.

7. Have Faith

Serena Williams' self-assurance over the tennis courts has allowed her to dominate. Her physique is not that of a "typical thin tennis player," but she accepts herself regardless while inspiring and encouraging other women. Having faith in every possible way in your life keeps you dominating and moving.

8. Shake It off Sooner

After qualifying for the Australian Open in 1998, Serena didn't have the best opening match, as she lost the first set. But she was not going down without a struggle. Her outstanding comebacks since then are well renowned. It's not over yet, just be present! You're still in it, and you'll have to battle for it.

9. Don't Give a Damn What Others Think

Williams has faced a lot of sexism and racism, mainly because of her physical appearance, which has been a significant factor in her domination. She has always been vocal on such criticism as well as encouraging women facing similar scepticism to heed not to what is said. As an aspiring female athlete, you can't afford the terror of being defined as "having too many muscles" and being mocked or labelled unattractive bring you down.

10. Believing in Oneself Can Be a Lonely Endeavour

People always doubted Serena's return after child delivery. But she always stated on several occasions that ignoring the odds and what others think is a critical component of overcoming hurdles and ultimately reaching success. When no one else believes in you, you have to believe in yourself.

Conclusion

Just like Serena Williams, no matter what your life's circumstances are, as an aspiring athlete or whatever your situation, keep your focus intact. Stay strong and always find a way of being a winner.

Chapter 6:

10 Habits of Unsuccessful People

Highly successful people (in any of the many ways that "success" can be defined) seem to recognize a few basic principles. The most important of these is that your energy, not your time, is restricted each day and must be carefully controlled.

Here are 10 of the most popular self-imposed blocks that have a troll on your success. If you come across one, use it as a cue to reevaluate, reflect, and change direction.

1. Worry of the Most Unlikely Outcome.

Despite its label as a "maladaptive trait," worrying has an evolutionary connection to intelligence. This is why, according to Jeremy Coplan, lead author of a study published of Frontiers in Evolutionary Neuroscience, effective people are naturally nervous.

Whatever the case may be, to work correctly, you must be able to distinguish between which fears are worth reacting to and which are your brain's attempt to "prepare" you for survival by conjuring up the most severe possible risk. This is an antiquated, animalistic mechanism that is useless in everyday life. Highly effective people should not spend their time worrying about the things that are least likely to happen.

2. Just Talking the Talk.

"I'm preparing to do this and that." What's better than announcing on social media that you're starting a business? Putting it into action.

Entrepreneur Derek Sivers argued in his 2010 TED talk, "Keep Your Goals to Yourself," that disclosing your intentions can be detrimental rather than inspiring. People will sometimes applaud you just for stating your purpose, he said, and this applause, ironically, may drain your motivation to carry out the plans you've just outlined.

"Psychotherapists have discovered that telling others your goal and having them embrace it is known as a 'social reality,'" Sivers explained in his talk. "The mind is deceived into believing it has already been accomplished. Then, after you've had your satisfaction, you're less likely to put in the necessary effort."

There's nothing wrong with expressing your happiness. However, try to keep your mouth shut before you have good news, not just good intentions.

3. Ruminating and Not Doing Anything About It.

Reflecting becomes ruminating as the intention to act dissolves in favor of constantly replaying certain situations or issues through your mind.

Self-awareness is common among highly successful individuals, or at least it should be. This means they devote a significant amount of time to reflecting on their behavior and experiences and determining how they can change. However, they do not waste mental energy pondering what went wrong rather than consciously modifying what needs to be changed to fix the issue.

4. Choosing the Wrong People To Spend Time With.

The people you hang out with can either inspire you to be your best self or bring out your worst traits. Spend time with people who can motivate you to make the changes you want to make in your life. Do you want to fail at that goal completely? If it's the case, spend time with people who gloat about their bad habits. People get their energy from each other. Always remember that you are the average of the 5 people that you spend most of your time with.

5. Being Resentful for Taking Time for Themselves.

People who have experienced any degree of success understand that it is a multi-faceted operation. You won't be able to work at your best if you're tired, undernourished, or experiencing some other sort of extreme imbalance in your life.

As a result, highly successful individuals are just as dedicated to relaxation and health as work and efficiency. They don't stress themselves up about how much they should have done in a three-day weekend or why they shouldn't take time off when they need it.

6. Constantly Concentrating on the Negative.

It's mind-boggling to focus on the negative aspects of life because it'll only make you feel worse. You don't have to believe that life is simple to concentrate on the positive. You should maintain a rational viewpoint without always pointing out the flaws in everything you see.

We've all met someone who is still complaining about something. "Ugh, it rained this morning, and my shoes were soaked through and through." Yes, that's a disappointment. You won't be able to affect the weather, unfortunately. You should put on a new pair of shoes if you want to.

It's fine if you're having a rough day; we're all irritable at times; everybody gets irritable now and then. However, you are living a poor life if you despise anything. That's what there is to it.

7. Justifying Their Place in Life.

Taking on exceptional work also elicits questions and, at times, judgments from those who don't believe in your project or are suspicious of its long-term viability. Constantly feeling the need to explain or justify your role in life, on the other hand, is not only exhausting but also unnecessary. Highly effective people understand that you can't get approval from people who don't want it.

8. Allowing Themselves To Be Sucked Into a State of Laziness.

We've all had times when we've been compelled to cancel plans. Leaving the house, even for something "fun," can feel like a Herculean task at times.

However, it is fresh and novel experiences that make life so beautiful. You aren't fully involved in your own life when you succumb to laziness, which is unfair to your friends, family, spouse, and those who want to share it with you.

9. Worrying That Isn't Essential and Unregulated Thought Patterns.

Worrying is among the most common ways people drain their energy doing. It is the act of anticipating the worst-case scenario and assuming that it is not only probable but most likely.

Worrying does not make you more equipped to deal with life's challenges instead, it makes you more likely to build your fears. You'd be surprised to learn that 99.9% of your worries were baseless and never "came true" if you made a list of everything you've ever worried about in your life.

If you just made a list of everything you didn't care about in life, you'd find that worrying didn't change anything; it just sapped your energy at the moment. The only thing it has done for you is that it made things more complicated, twisted, and less fun. It is not only ineffective, but completely pointless as well. Highly successful people learn to concentrate on something else rather than spend their time worrying about what could go wrong.

10.There Is Just Too Much Optimistic Thought.

It's self-evident that no one achieves remarkable success without first confronting destructive thought patterns. What's less evident is that highly successful people don't partake in excessive positive thinking, which can be arbitrary, distorted, and even distracting in excess. Worse, they set themselves up for failure or disappointment by thinking too positively. Instead, highly successful people understand the power of neutral thought, which means they don't try to make life into something.

Conclusion

If you don't want to be an unsuccessful person, you need to make a conscious effort to avoid doing these things. Focus on the habits that would bring you positive change instead, which we will discuss in another segment.

Chapter 7:

10 Habits That Can Ruin Your Day

Habits are the building blocks of our day. No matter how you spin it, either way, every detail matters.

The little actionable habits eventually sets you up to a either having a fulfilling day, or one that you have just totally wasted away. Nothing is as bad as destructive habits as they sabotage your daily productivity. Slowly, you slip further and further until it's too late when you've realized the damage that they have done to your life.

Bad habits are insidious! They drag down your life, lowers down your levels of accuracy, and make your performance less creative and stifling. It is essential, not only for productivity, to gain control of your bad habits. AS Grenville Kleiser once noted, "Constant self-discipline and self-control help you develop greatness of character." Nonetheless, it is important to stop and ask: what do you need today to get rid of or change? Sure, you can add or adjust new skills into your daily life.

Below are ten persistent habits that can ruin your day's success and productivity.

1. Hitting The Snooze Button.

Your mind, while you sleep, moves through a comprehensive series of cycles, the last one alerting you to wake up. While you crave for ten more minutes of sleep as the alarm goes off, what do you do? You whacked the snooze button. We're all guilty of this! If you don't suck it up, rip off the cover and start your morning, the rest of your day will be flawed. How do you expect your day to be strong once you don't start it off strong? You will feel far more optimistic, strong and fully prepared when you wake up without hitting the snooze button. So avoid the snooze button at any cost if you want a productive day ahead!

2. Wasting Your "Getting Ready" Hours.

You might need to reconsider the scrolling of Instagram and Facebook or the inane program you put on behind the scenes while preparing. These things have a time and place to partake in them – for example when you've accomplished your day's work and need some time to unwind and relax; however the time isn't now. Your morning schedule ought to be an interaction that prepares and energizes you for the day ahead. The objective is to accomplish something that animates your mind within the first hour of being conscious, so you can be more inventive, invigorated, gainful, and connected with all through the entire day! Avoiding this sweeps you away from normalizing the worst habit you might have: distraction. Instead, give yourself a chance to breathe the fine morning, anticipate the day's wonder and be thankful for whatever you have.

3. Failing To Prioritize Your Breakfast.

Energizing your day is essential if you wish for a very productive day. Energizing your body system requires that you prioritize eating your breakfast. However, the contents of your breakfast must entail something that will ensure that your day is not slowed down by noon. This means a blend of high - fiber foods such as proteins and healthy must be incorporated. Avoid taking too many sugars and heavy starches. The goal is to satiate and energize your body for the day.

4. Ruminating on the Problems of Yesterday And Negativity.

Don't take yesterday's problems to your new day if you want to start your day off right. If the day before you had difficult meetings and talks and you woke up ruminating about your horrific experiences, leave that negativity at your doorway. Moreover, if the problem you are lamenting about have been solved, then you shouldn't dwell on the past. Research suggests that we usually encounter more positive than negative events in a day. Still, often your mind concentrates on the negative due to a subconscious distortion called the negative distortion. By choosing not to focus on negative events and thinking about what's going well, you can learn to take advantage of the strength of the positive events around us. Raising negativity only increases stress. Let go of it and get on without it!

5. Leaving Your Day To Randomness.

Do not let stuff just simply happen to you; do it. Failure to create a structured day leads to a totally random day. A random day lacking direction, focus, and efficiency. Distractions will also creep into your day more readily because you have allowed randomness to happen to you. Instead, have a clear and precise list of what you need to focus for the day. This serves as a framework and a boundary for you to work within. Another thing you should consider is to spend your first 90 minutes on the most thoughtful and important task for the day. This allows you to know the big things out right at the beginning, reducing your cognitive burden for the rest of the day.

6. Becoming Involved With the Overview.

How frequently have you woken up, and before you can stretch and grin, you groan pretty much all the have-to for now and the fragmented musts from yesterday? This unhealthy habit will ruin your great day ahead. Know and understand these are simply contemplations. You can decide to recalibrate by pondering all you must be thankful for and searching for the splendid focuses in your day. Shift thinking, and you'll begin the day empowered.

7. Overscheduling and Over-Engagement.

People tend to underestimate how long things take with so many things to do. This habit of overscheduling and over-engagement can quickly lead to burn out. Always ensure that you permit extra time and energy for the unforeseen. Take regular breaks and don't overcommit to other people. This gives you more freedom for yourself and you won't be running the risk of letting others down by not turning up. Try not to overestimate what you can complete, so you won't feel like a disappointment. Be sensible and practical with your scheduling. Unexpectedly and eventually, you'll complete more.

8. Postponing or Discarding the Tough Tasks.

We have a restricted measure of mental energy, and as we exhaust this energy, our dynamic and efficiency decrease quickly. This is called decision exhaustion. Running the bad habit of postponing and disregarding the tough tasks will trigger this reaction in us. At the point when you put off extreme assignments till late in the day because they're scary, you deplete more and more of your mental resources. To beat choice weariness, you should handle complex assignments toward the beginning of the day when your brain is new.

9. Failure To Prioritize Your Self-Care.

Work, family commitments, and generally talking of the general obligations give almost everyone an awesome excuse to let your self-care rehearses pass by the wayside. Achievement-oriented minds of individuals see how basic self-care is to their expert achievement. Invest energy doing things that bring you delight and backing your psychological and actual wellbeing. "Success" doesn't exclusively apply to your finances or expert accomplishments.

10.Waiting for the Easier Way Out / Waiting for the Perfect Hack of Your Life.

The most noticeably awful everyday habit is trusting that things will occur and for a chance to thump at your entryway. As such, you become an inactive onlooker, not a proactive part of your own life. Once in a while, it shows itself as the quest for simple little-known techniques. Rather than getting down to work, ineffective individuals search how to take care of job quicker for quite a long time. Try not to begin with a #lifehack search on the internet unless it really does improve your productivity without sacrificing the necessary steps you need to take each day to achieve holistic success.

✓ Merging It All Together

A portion of these habits may appear to be minor, yet they add up. Most amount to an individual decision between immediate pleasures and enduring ones. The most exceedingly awful propensity is forgetting about what matters to you. Always remember that you are just one habit away from changing you life forever.

Chapter 8:

How To Succeed In Life

"You can't climb the ladder of success with your hands in your pocket."

Every day that you're living, make a habit of making the most out of it. Make a habit of winning today. Don't dwell on the past, don't worry about the future. You just have to make sure that you're winning today. Move a little forward every day; take a little step every day. And when you're giving your fruitful efforts, you're making sure you're achieving your day, then you start to built confidence within yourselves. Confidence is when you close your eyes at night and see a vision, a dream, a goal, and you believe that you're going to achieve it. When you're doing things, when you're productive the whole day, then that long journey will become short in a matter of time.

Make yourself a power list for each day. Take a sheet of paper, write Monday on top of it and then write five critical, productive, actionable tasks that you're going to do that day. After doing the task, cross it off. Repeat the process every day of every week of every month till you get closer to achieving your goals, your dreams. It doesn't matter if you're doing the same tasks every day or how minor or major they are; what matters is that it's creating momentum in things that you've believed you couldn't do. And as soon as the momentum gets completed, you start to believe that you can do something. You eventually stop writing your tasks down because now they've become your new habits. You need a reminder for them. You don't need to cross them off because you're going to do them. The power list helps you win the day. You're stepping out of your comfort zone, doing something that looks uncomfortable for starters, but while doing this, even for a year, you will see yourself standing five years from where you're standing today.

Decide, commit, act, succeed, repeat. If you want to be an inspiration to others, a motivator to others, impact others somehow, you have to self-evaluate certain perceptions and think that'll help you change the way you see yourself and the world. Perseverance, hard-working, and consistency would be the keywords if one were to achieve success in life. You just have to keep yourself focused on your ultimate goal. You will fall a hundred times. There's always stumbling on the way. But if you have the skill, the power, the instinct to get yourself back up every time you fall, and to dig yourself out of the whole, then no one can stop you. You have to control the situation, Don't ever let the situation control you. You're living life exactly as it should be. If you don't like what you're living in, then consider changing the aspects. The person you are right now versus the person you want to be in the future, there's only a fine line between the two that you have to come face-to-face with.

Your creativity is at most powerful the moment you open your eyes and start your day. That's when you get the opportunity to steer your emotions and thoughts in the direction that you want them to go, not the other way around. Every failure is a step closer to success. We won't succeed on the first try, and we will never have it perfect by trying it only once. But we can master the art of not giving up. We dare to take risks. If we never fail, we never get the chance of getting something we never had. We can never taste the fruits of success without falling. The difference between successful people and those who aren't successful is the point of giving up.

Success isn't about perfection. Instead, it's about getting out of bed each day, clearing the dust off you, and thinking like a champion, a winner, going on about your day, being productive, and making the most out of it. Remember that the mind controls your body; your body doesn't hold your mind. You have to make yourself mentally tough to overcome the fears and challenges that come in the way of your goals. As soon as you get up in the morning, start thinking about anything or anyone that you're grateful for. Your focus should be on making yourself feel good and confident enough to get yourself through the day.

The negative emotions that we experience, like pain or rejection, or frustration, cannot always make our lives miserable. Instead, we can consider them as our most incredible friends that'll drive us to success. When people succeed, they tend to party. When they fail, they tend to ponder. And the pondering helps us get the most victories in our lives. You're here, into another day, still breathing fine, that means you got another chance, to better yourself, to be able to right your wrongs. Everyone has a more significant potential than the roles they put themselves in.

Trust yourself always. Trust your instinct—no matter what or how anyone thinks. You're perfectly capable of doing things your way. Even if they go wrong, you always learn something from them. Don't ever listen to the naysayers. You've probably heard a million times that you can't do this and you can't do that, or it's never even been done before. So what? So what if no one has ever done it before. That's more of the reason for you to do it since you'll become the first person to do it. Change that 'You can't' into 'Yes, I definitely can.' Muhammad Ali, one of the greatest boxers to walk on the face of this planet, was once asked, 'how many sit-ups do you do?' to which he replied, 'I don't count my sit-ups. I only start counting when it starts hurting. When I feel pain, that's when I start counting because that's when it really counts.' So we get a wonderful lesson to work tirelessly and shamelessly if we were to achieve our dreams. Dr. Arnold Schwarzenegger beautifully summed up life's successes in 6 simple rules; Trust yourself, Break some rules, Don't be afraid to fail, Ignore the naysayers, Work like hell, And give something back.

CHAPTER 9:

10 Habits that Make You More Attractive

Being attractive does not necessarily connote physical appearance. More than the physical appearance, attraction renders the mental, emotional, and spiritual energy irresistible to others. Some people radiate with their energy and confidence regardless of whether they have money, looks, or are socially connected. These people are just irresistible, and you will find that people will always approach them for advice, help, or even long-term companionships. What makes them more attractive? Their sense of self-worth is always from within their souls as contrasted with how they look from outside. They don't seek validation from others- but find it within themselves.

However, this is not genetically connected, but a habit that we can build within ourselves. You need to pursue and maintain such habits for the benefit of a greater you.

Here are 10 habits that make you more attractive:

1. **Connect With People More Deeply.**

Attractive people are always likable people, and being likable is a skill. Being likable means that you should be interested in hearing others out rather than spending all the time thinking and talking about yourself. As entrepreneur Jim Rohn puts it- "Irresistible or likable people possess an authentic personality that enables them to concentrate more on those around them." This requires that you are in most cases over yourself, meaning that you don't spend more time only thinking about yourself.

To have this habit going on in you, try to take conversations seriously. Put that phone down and listen! Learn what those around you are into - Ask questions, enquire about their dreams, fears, preferences, and views on life. Focus on what is being said rather than what the response is or what impact that might have on you. Always aim to make others everyone feel valued and important.

2. **Treat Everyone With Respect.**

Being polite and unfailingly respectful is the key to being likable. If you are always rude to others, you will find that over time people will tend to avoid you. You should strive to not only be respectful to someone you know and like, but also to strangers that you come across with. Attractive people treat everyone with the same respect they deserve bearing in mind that no one is better.

3. **Follow the Platinum Rule.**

The commonly known version of the golden rule is that you should treat others the same way you want them to treat you. This comes with a major flaw: the assumption that everyone aspires to be treated similarly. The rule ignores the fact people are different and are motivated differently. For instance, one person's love for public attention is another's person's execrate. However, you can opt for this flaw by adopting the platinum rule instead. The notion is that you should only treat others as they want to be treated. Attractive people are good at reading others and quickly adjust to their style and behavior, and as a result, they can treat them in a way that makes them feel comfortable.

4. **Don't Try Too Hard To Put an Impression.**

Attractive people who are easily likable don't try too hard to impress. Liking someone comes naturally, and it depends on their personality. Hence if you spend most of the time bragging about your success or smartness, you are simply harming yourself without knowing it. People who try too hard to be liked are not likable at all. Instead they come across as narcissistic and arrogant. If you wish to be an attractive person choose to be humble and down-to-earth instead. People will see your worth with their own two eyes.

5. **Forgive and Learn From Your Mistakes.**

Learning from our mistakes is synonymous with self-improvement. It is proven that psychological traits are essential in human mating or relationships, meaning that both intelligence and kindness are key. Being intelligent, in this case, doesn't necessarily mean the PHDs or Degrees. It means that a person can demonstrate intelligence by learning from mistakes they make and handling the same well. You demonstrate this also by being kind to yourself whenever you make a mistake and avoiding the same mistake in the future. Attractive people know how to not take themselves too seriously and to have a laugh at themselves once in a while.

6. Smile Often

People tend to bond unconsciously with the body language portrayed while conversing. If you are geared towards making people more attracted to you, smile at them when conversing or talking to them. A smile makes other people feel comfortable in conversations, and in turn, they do the same to you. The feeling is remarkably good!

7. Likable People Are Authentic and Are Persons of Integrity.

People are highly attractive to realness. Attractive people portray who they are. Nobody has to expend energy or brainpower guessing their objective or predicting what they'll do next. They do this because they understand that no one likes a fake. People will gravitate toward you if you are genuine because it is easy to rely on you. On the flip side, it is also easy to resist getting close to someone if you don't know who they really are or how they actually feel.

People with high integrity are desirable because they walk their talk. Integrity is a straightforward idea, but it isn't easy to put into action. To show honesty every day, attractive people follow through with this trait. They refrain from gossiping about others and they do the right thing even if it hurts them to do so.

8. Recognize and Differentiate Facts and

Opinions.

Attractive people can deal gracefully and equally with divisive subjects and touchy issues. They don't shy away from expressing their views, but they clarify that they are just that: opinions, not facts. So, whenever you in a heated discussion, be it on politics or other areas with your peers, it is important to understand that people are different and are just as intelligent as you are. Everyone holds a different opinion; while facts always remain facts. Do not confuse the two to be the same.

9. Take Great Pleasure in The Little Things

Choose joy and gratitude in every moment – No matter if you are feeling sad, fearful, or happy. People who appreciates life for its up and downs will always appear attractive to others. Choose to see life as amazing and carefully approach it with joy and gratitude – Spread positive vibes and attract others to you that are also positive in nature. View obstacles as temporary, not inescapable. Everyone has problems, but it is how you deal with it each day that is important here. Optimistic people will always come out on top.

10. Treating friendships with priority.

True friendships are a treasure. When you take your time and energy to nourish true friendships, you will naturally develop others skills necessary to sustain all forms of relationships in your life. People will always gravitate to a person who is genuinely friendly and caring. They want to be a part of this person's life because it brings them support and joy. Take these friendships with you to the distance.

Bonus Tip: Do Your Best to Look Good.

There is a huge difference between presentation and vanity. An attractive person will always make efforts to look presentable to others. This is comparable to tidying up the house before you receive visitors - which is a sign of gratitude to others. Don't show up sloppily to meetups and parties; this will give others the impression that you don't care about how you look which may put off others from approaching you. Always try your best in every situation.

Conclusion: Bringing it all in

Attractive people don't get these habits simply floating over their beds. They have mastered those attractive characteristics and behaviors consciously or subconsciously - which anyone can easily adopt.

You have to think about other people more than you think about yourself, and you have to make others feel liked, appreciated, understood, and seen. Note, the more you concentrate on others, the more attractive you will appear and become without even trying.

CHAPTER 10:

10 Habits of Jack Ma

It takes a special person to amass a total net worth of more than $20 billion through hard work and keeping a sense of perspective. Alibaba, one of world's largest e-commerce online platforms, Ceo and founder, Jack Ma is one of the world's wealthiest people, but his success hasn't clouded his strategic direction. Jack Ma's success habits will truly inspire you whether you are an aspiring billionaire or you're a small-business entrepreneur.

To grow his e-commerce business, Jack overcame all difficulties. He had a rough upbringing in communist China. He also failed the college admissions exams twice and was turned down by more than a dozen businesses. He had previously created two failed Internet businesses. However, the third time, Alibaba took off swiftly.

Here are 10 things you can grasps from Jack Ma success journey:

1. Giving Up is Failing

Jack Ma is one person who understands the meaning of failure, as it started in his early days. He founded two companies which terribly failed before the success of Alibaba. For Ma, giving up is failure.

Give your grind your best shot even when the struggle is real. Failing shouldn't make you give up, instead make sure you see the goal through to the end. Hardship is your learning lesson, and understanding its lessons is the key to fortune.

2. Let Your Initiative Impact on Society Positively

Ma created his vision focusing on its impactful influence on consumers. He also notes that consumer's happiness should be the end goal rather than the profits.

Let your entrepreneurial path be the reason why people's lives are improving. This results will be in long-term-positive business relationships.

3. What's Matters Is Where You Finish

Your humble beginnings shouldn't prevent you from taking chances. Your spirit, toughness, grit, and fortitude will tell whether or not you'll succeed.

What matters is whether you are putting much effort as needed and this will tell how determined you are to succeed. Dig in your heels, like Jack Ma, and give every opportunity your all.

4. Act Swiftly

According to Jack Ma, you must be extremely quick in seizing opportunities. To win in the end, you must first be off the starting line. You must also be quick to recover from and learn from mistakes. Grab an opportunity that is in your line of sight as soon as you see it and work with it before anyone else does. This will elevate you above your competitors, who are merely competent.

5. Persistence

Ma believes that leaders must be tenacious and with a clear vision. Understanding what you want and having the drive to pursue it will not only put you on the path to success, but will also inspire those around you to work hard to achieve their goals. Ma's business concept is around taking pleasure in one's job and refusing to accept no for an answer.

6. Foresightedness

A good leader, according to Jack Ma, should have foresight. As a leader, it's good that you're always one step ahead of the competition by anticipating how decisions will be implemented before others. Invest your time in developing creative strategies while intensifying a trait where you always follow a knowledge-based intuition.

7. Take a risk

Ma founded Alibaba Group, a very successful conglomerate of internet enterprises, in the face of skepticism from potential investors. The perfect time to take risks, is when you are pursuing your chosen goal path-when criticism is at its core.

8. Be Prepared to Fail

Jack Ma is no stranger to failure. He applied to college three times before being accepted. He created two unsuccessful companies before success of Alibaba. Even KFC didn't think he was a good fit.

When you give up on your first try, you are turning your life around. As probably you'll move on to something else while ending your dreams.

9. Take Chances When You're Still Young

Ma believes that if you are not wealthy by the age of 35, you have squandered your youth. Take use of your youth's vitality and imagination by succumbing to your goal and pursuing it.

Accept and learn from every opportunity that comes your way while you're still young. Grab every opportunity and make best of it by giving it your all. Your ability to pick up any job will help you develop tenancy.

10. Live life

Ma has a reputation for not taking things too seriously. Despite his hectic schedule, he always finds time to relax and enjoy life. If you work your whole life, you will undoubtedly come to regret it.

Conclusion

Jack Ma is one of most inspiring person in the world. His struggle way up and desire for wealth continues to inspire. Through his experience, Jack Ma demonstrates how as an entrepreneur, you can bring ambition to life.